ABOUT LEARNING

ABOUT LEARNING

THEORY THEN AND NOW

LOUIS EVERSTINE

Library of Congress Control Number:		2014911372
ISBN:	Hardcover	978-1-4990-4107-1
	Softcover	978-1-4990-4108-8
	eBook	978-1-4990-4106-4

This book was printed in the United States of America.

Photograph of the author: André Monjoin
Text preparation: Rana K. Soinski
Production assistance: Andy Maxwell, Nelson Boyd

Rev. date: 09/10/2014

To order additional copies of this book, contact:
Xlibris LLC
1-888-795-4274
www.Xlibris.com
Orders@Xlibris.com
626879

CONTENTS

For Daphne Hereward, my muse of Oxford

PREFACE

Soon after I began graduate school in Psychology at the University of Pittsburgh, several home truths became clear. One was that there was, between experimental psychologists and clinical psychologists, "a vast gulf fixed." Decades later, this chasm still exists. Some psychologists consider themselves to be "scientists," and to have at least a collegial relationship with physicists and cancer researchers. Whether or not the connection is valid is not for me to say. The salient fact is that research-oriented psychologists are snobbish about the "purity" of their discipline, as opposed to that of fuzzy-headed clinicians. In their view, the practitioner is awash in a subjective view of people and what makes them tick.

Another lesson that I learned, early in the graduate school experience, was that psychologists are seen, by psychiatrists, as second-class citizens. For my internship, I was assigned to Western Psychiatric Institute of the School of Medicine. The Chairman of the Department of Psychology in that hospital was Dr. Roy Hamlin, scholar, gentleman, and master clinician. He told me one day that, by watching a patient walk from the door of his office to the chair by his desk, he could make a correct diagnosis of the person. I never doubted it. He also told me that, although he preferred doing therapy instead of intake interviews, he could have no more than one therapy client, and only if supervised by one of the psychiatrists. Further, interns were not permitted to have therapy clients under any circumstances; our role was limited to giving tests and writing testing reports. This was fifty-plus years ago, and how times have changed: today, psychiatrists conduct interviews and prescribe drugs. Psychologists do therapy.

A further complication in the graduate training experience was that the Psychology Department of the University was, at that time, an outpost of Skinnerian conditioning theory. Rats and monkeys were trained to press levers, and the brains of some monkeys were examined to find possible neural correlates to learning. Learning theory pervaded courses on any subject and efforts were made to devise training methods in various academic fields employing "programmed learning," in which "prompts" influenced responses that, if correct, produced "reinforcement."

Even though we intended to take up careers as clinicians and never set foot in a laboratory, my colleagues and I were compelled to listen to, and regurgitate on tests, hours on end of "operant" ideology. I played the game, but couldn't get my head around what seemed to be a logical conundrum in the theory, namely that a reinforcing stimulus *following* a response could increase the likelihood that the response would occur again. The logical choices were obvious: either the response would be more likely or less likely to occur again.

Figuring out which of those outcomes was plausible required finding out what causes a response to occur in the first place—*before* being followed by a reinforcing stimulus. Skinner's theory is silent on this point, resting on the assumption that *something* must have caused an initial response, but that what it was is irrelevant—no need to find out. Paradoxes and conundrums such as these are the subjects of the analysis of theory that this book presents.

Turning from the theoretical to the practical, it goes without saying that, if we can discover how people learn, we can find ways to teach them. This book reviews more than a century of efforts by psychologists and other scientists to analyze, distill, and synthesize our accumulated knowledge of the learning process *per se*. How much have *we* learned? For example, how does a child learn to write an algorithm or learn the nuances of playing a violin? How does the child of two learn language, or how does a person of 30 learn a foreign tongue? Socrates was not the first to seek the ideal teaching method, and modern educators have evolved their own concepts of instilling knowledge—with little help from psychologists. For their part, parents in the ultimate classroom, the family, rely on methods that originated long before Lincoln studied by the light of a tallow candle. These pages trace our understanding of how people learn, from the Nineteenth Century to the present.

ACKNOWLEDGEMENTS

Much that I learned about how people learn was first given to me in graduate school at the University of Pittsburgh in the nineteen-fifties. There, I was lucky enough to be taught by the Professors Roy Hamlin and Bill Bendig, who encouraged me to question what, in Psychology, was at the time Revealed Truth. I took some courses by the Philosopher Oliver Reiser, whose vision ranged far beyond persuading rats to push levers; nor was this scholar concerned with human skill-learning, but was a humanist through and through. In England, Alan Watson at Cambridge and Ted Crossman at Oxford were great hosts and inspiring role models.

These were my mentors and friends of student days, and I shall never forget them. The original version of this book was typed, in its entirety, by Daphne Hereward. An Oxford graduate in Classics, she had stayed on in Oxford and sustained herself in poverty by freelance typing. Here is one of her published poems, written originally in Greek:

PTOLEMY

I know myself a man, short-lived and mortal,
But when I track the courses of the sky,
I find myself rise up to heaven's portal,
And for those moments feel eternity.

Later in life, Ms. Hereward volunteered to become a teacher of little children in Ghana. After many years living alone, she died there. I could not have written this book without her.

The text of this revision of the book was prepared by Rana K. Soinski, with her characteristically precise attention to detail.

I. HISTORY

Psychology entered the laboratory in 1879 at Leipzig and if a dog were to measure its years it would be found to have achieved the age of nineteen. It is realistic to expect that this science has left infancy and childhood behind: it will soon be mobile with energy, awkward by growth, troublous and strident in its advancement toward maturity. The best dreams of Psychology are yet to come.

The paradox of Psychology is not its rapid development as a modern experimental science. Its late beginning conferred advantages the histories of other sciences do not share: from the start it could with heightened awareness oppose all metaphysical influences; from the start, it had the most assiduous empirical approaches and practices as examples before it to be imitated by incorporation. Psychology's paradox occurred when the young science put aside its original subject and made its field of investigation entirely new. Revolutions of compelling significance have transformed several major sciences in this century, but the massive reconstruction of Psychology served to award this science much of the mystique of the changeling.

In a Presidential address to a Convention of the American Psychological Association, D.O. Hebb described forty years of revolution in Psychology. Hebb referred to the period spanning the emergence of Thorndike as a major theorist and the publication, in 1938, of the *The Behavior of Organisms*, by B.F. Skinner. That revolt was behaviorism. Hebb's address began with a citation of praise for the "thoroughgoing behavioristic mode of thinking" which the revolution had established in the young science. The new conception of the task and eventual purposes of this science effected a slow yet complete transformation. In modern Psychology, behaviorism has no challenger.

A science of behavior rejected a science of the mind. By this reversal, the first subjects of psychological research ceased to exist. It is clear that the intention under which Psychology originated was that a proven and popular empirical determinism would accomplish the understanding of mental events. Mind—subject of the speculation of centuries—was to be examined, dissected. Causal laws of thought were to be produced by laboratory investigations analogous to those which had discovered the characteristics of a vacuum. It was the intention of Wundt's Leipzig laboratory to conduct experiments on mentality in terms, Boring wrote, of "formal elements, like sensation, which have attributes of their own and which are connected by association." (1950, p.329) Introspection was to analyze—much as chromatography separates by adsorption—the properties of which experience is compounded.

Then, with the new century, a categorical re-organization of the science began. How this came about was described by various historians. (Hilgard and Marquis, 1940; Spence, 1956; Boring, 1957). For what reason did the behaviorist thesis take form, have its effect, take hold? The ideological springs which assured the success of the revolution were obscured by this passage in Hebb's address:

> The essence of the psychological revolution was the serious, systematic application of the stimulus-response formula to all aspects of behavior, with a consequent development of rigor in experimental analysis. (1960, p.736)

It is not precisely clear from this statement that the prime aim, the initial commitment of the early behaviorists was to bring into Psychology at last a tough-minded empiricism that in the nineteenth century it had lacked. At first, behaviorism was not so much a revised conception of learning—nor even a thoroughgoing psychological theory—than an injunction that psychologists abandon one way of doing science for another.

There was no question but that Psychology was caught up in a struggle to be taken seriously as a science. Wundt wrote of the requisite approach Psychology would have to adopt toward the problems of its subject, comparing this with the requirements of physics in coming to terms with demands of scientific method:

> . . . this form of Psychology cannot admit any fundamental difference between the methods of Psychology and those of natural science. It has, therefore, sought above all to cultivate *experimental* methods which shall lead to just such an exact analysis of psychical processes as that which the explanatory natural sciences undertake in the case of natural phenomenal,

the only differences being those which arise
from the diverse points of view. (1902, p.10)

Much later, J.B. Watson reflected on his own
accomplishment by making this synonymous statement:

> Behaviorism, as I tried to develop it . . . was
> an attempt to do one thing—to apply to the
> experimental study of man the same kind of
> procedure and the same language of description
> that many research men had found useful for
> so many years in the study of animals lower
> than man. (1930, p.V)

Experimentalists thus were committed to experimental
rigor—their methodological inspirations were to be taken
by analogy from other sciences. To make Psychology
pure by association, both theorists dispatched what was
"classical" to match Psychology with whatever borrowed
scientific model that held their favor. Yet as for Wundt the
"last and most general" end of Psychology was to discover
the *"laws of psychical phenomena"* (1902, p.31), Watson's
contribution in its turn forced that summation to be
cancelled.

The removal of the psychic from Psychology became
an automatic constituent of its scientification. Without
the stringent demands this quest for scientific orthodoxy
would impose—nor the sweeping character of the
excisions from Psychology this reform would require—
the problem of consciousness was cut away. According
to Watson,

> Behaviorism claims that consciousness is
> neither a definite nor a usable concept. The

behaviorist, who has been trained always as an experimentalist, holds . . . that belief in the existence of consciousness goes back to ancient days of superstition and magic . . . that no Psychology which included the religious mind-body problem could ever arrive at verifiable conclusions. (1930, pp. 2, 5)

To make a science in which conclusions were demonstrable, replicable, and what was to be known as *operationally* definable—in a word, verifiable—behaviorism invented behavior. For if Psychology was to be strictly a science, then it required rigid application of scientific method. If Psychology was to be modeled after those sciences which took as their subject animals lower in the phylogenetic scale than man, to what other event could its examinations be put than to behavior? Scientism and animalism thus transformed child of mind to child of act:

1. Summarizing, Psychology began because: the study of the mind was important; philosophical speculations had failed to provide adequate explanations of mental events; the methods of nineteenth century science were available.
2. Psychology abandoned study of the mind because: a mistake was discovered—no rigorous science could provide an explanation of mental events; sciences were required to be rigorous.
3. Psychology became a science of behavior because: rigorous sciences of lower organisms had been developed; rightly or wrongly—animals only act.

How Psychology moved from this point of rebirth to its position as a stimulus-response science of behavior is the subject of the following pages.

The concept of the response as a functional correlate of a prior stimulus can be understood as an inevitable result of the decision to reduce—or refine—mental science to behavior science. The path followed by Psychology to the response has been traced; it was established by fiat:

> The behaviorist asks: Why don't we make what we can *observe* the real field of Psychology? Let us limit ourselves to things that can be observed, and formulate laws concerning only those things. Now what can we observe? We can observe *behavior—what the organism does or says.* (Watson, 1930, p. 6)

The earliest formulation—in 1912—of Watson's dogma served only to solidify the already growing significance of the overt, measurable muscle movement as a unitary psychological datum. The notion of a response Psychology was not new. Watson was an adamant scientist and skillful organizer; he was an executor and not an innovator of the behaviorist revolution. What is striking is that, by this doctrine, responses as primal elements of psychological description and analysis stand as evidence of the intention of the science to study events at the *periphery* of the organism. This touchstone—response—will be analyzed comprehensively in chapters to follow. It is introduced in this preliminary discussion to show that behaviorism took Psychology as far as it was possible to go outside of the organism—in effect, to the nerve endings supplying major muscle groups.

The response, as terminal event in a chain of causally related events, had previously been considered to be the result of one of two sets of determiners: (1) mental events as causes; (2) physiological events as causes. These share the obscurity of occurrence *within* the responding organism. Thus they were ripe for discard. On the causative side of behavior, the stimulus came to be regarded not as the initiator of a series of processes of which mind or body were mediational events; rather, the chain was designed to pass them by. Spence has described the stimulus as, in itself, a sufficient cause of the response:

> The physical sciences . . . deal only with events of an extra-organic origin—i.e., those received through the exteroceptors. The data of classical Psychology, on the other hand, were regarded as involving primarily sense events initiated through the interoceptors. The latter were regarded as being stimulated by such internal mental activities as thinking, desiring, emotional reactions, perceiving, etc., and hence were thought of as providing primary data . . .

> It is apparent . . . that these internally initiated experiences differ rather markedly from the externally aroused ones in the extent to which they are publicly controllable and communicable . . . if we can judge from the interminable disagreements of the introspective psychologists themselves, this class of experiences does not meet . . . the requirements of social verification and acceptance demanded by the scientist. It was

in the face of this difficulty that Watson made
his suggestion that the psychologist, like all
other scientists, should confine himself to
those segments of his experience which have
their origin in extra-organic conditions. (1948,
pp. 67, 68)

This description contains a vital key to the fundamental
sources of modern Psychology. To say that "extra-organic
conditions" were—by scientific necessity—those
conditions that were to serve as causes for psychological
events is to express criteria for the dominant and pervasive
psychological theories of the twentieth century.

Relationships between organism and environment
contain infinite sources of potential variation. A
Psychology charged with the responsibility of explaining
relationships of such complexity required an economical
employment of its scientific energies. If any direct—
one to one—relation could be described with precision
by the science, it was epitomized by those occasions in
which response changes follow upon stimulus changes.
That is, the stimulus-response formula could best be
fitted to explanations of how a given response varied as
a function of a specific environmental event. This states
the traditional formulation of the psychological subject of
learning. Continuing his description of the work of the
early behaviorists, Hebb reminded us that:

They made learning the fundamental issue in
Psychology, as it still is, by the simple device
of denying that there was anything else to be
accounted for . . . the only connected, consistent
attempts at explanations in Psychology are to

be found in one form or other of learning theory. (1960, pp. 736, 738)

Behavioral modification became the problem to which the stimulus-response formula was the key. How the responses of an organism changes as a function of X. This pre-eminent puzzle remains the final legacy of the behaviorist revolution.

As its nuclear unit of discovery, modern Psychology has chosen the response. What can be measured is an act; not an act as the writing of a symphony can be considered an integrated act; rather, as the placing of a mark of ink upon a page is an act; better, the activation of muscles required to move a hand holding a pen toward a page. Nothing is more measurable and at the same time more variable about a person than this.

Then a person is his or her acts. Modern Psychology is an ideology promulgated to educate converts in that belief. Since B.F. Skinner has been moved to poetry to express this liturgy, let him explain it in verse:

> Yes, 'all's behavior
> —and the rest is naught' . . .
> Let not the strong
> Be cozened
> By *Is* and *Isn't*
> *Was* and *Wasn't*.
> Truth's to be sought
> In *Does* and *Doesn't*.
> Decline
> *To be* . . .
> (from "For Ivor Richards," Skinner, 1962, pp. 43, 44)

There is more error in that creed than wisdom. It is the task of this book to reach and expose the source of that error. It is to be found masked by postulates of a theory. The masks are ripped apart by sense, not data. The ruling dogma of modern Psychology need not be refuted by empirical proofs. It can be explained away.

The act is everything. It can be a finger moving one quantifiable dimension of time/space. It is a gesture. It is a word—any word the human organism can write or speak. The act is the person talking out against the dark—performing in defiance of nothingness. It defines self. A Psychology of acts is the logical culmination of the reconstruction in psychological method that ended in 1938. The search for causes of acts has dominated Psychology since then.

Organismic variables have had persistence in psychological theory and research; their decline to insignificance did not at first develop as rapidly as this passage suggests:

> A survey of the research literature since the beginning of experimental Psychology will reveal the extraordinary extent to which the interests of psychologists have turned . . . less and less [to the] class of relations which involve, as one of the members, physiological and anatomical variables. . . . With the advent of the functional and behavioristic viewpoints . . . physiological research declined markedly until it now represents a relatively small proportion of the total research activity of psychologists. (Spence, 1956, p. 17)

Watson's initial proposals for the new Psychology had attempted to establish a working liaison with physiological sciences—at least those which investigated metabolic processes. This projected alliance was manifest in Watson's definition of "stimulus":

> By stimulus we mean any object in the general environment or any change in the *tissues themselves* due to the physiological condition of the animal. (1930, p. 6)

This shows that Watson conceived of the stimulus as occupying twin loci, outside the organism and inside it. It meant that his S-R formula incorporated stimuli produced by tissue-needs. The latter required explanations which could only be provided by the data and constructs of physiology.

On the response side of the equation, Watson took a somewhat more complicated position with respect to relationships between psychological and physiological explanations; he described behaviorism as:

> . . . a natural science that takes the whole field of human adjustments as its own. Its closest scientific companion is physiology . . . It is different from physiology only in the grouping of its problems, not in fundamentals . . . Physiology is particularly interested in the functioning of parts of the animal . . . Behaviorism, on the other hand, while it is intensely interested in all of the functioning of these parts, is intrinsically interested in what the whole animal will *do* from morning to night and from night to morning. (1930, p. 11)\

As for those physicalist formulations to be derived from the data of neurology, neuroanatomy, etc., Watson found them especially misleading for the purposes of Psychology. By answering in the negative his own question "Should we as behaviorists be especially interested in the central nervous system?," Watson put aside neurophysiology by the following criteria:

> For the behaviorist the nervous system is, first, a part of the body—no more mysterious than muscles and glands; second, it is a specialized body mechanism that enables its possessor to react more quickly and in a more integrated way with muscles and glands when acted upon by a given stimulus than would be the case if no nervous system were present . . . The behaviorist then has to be vitally interested in the nervous system but only as an integral part of the whole body. (1930, pp. 49, 50)

More conservative theorists than Watson have struggled to arrive at a decision about how much of physiology to include in their formulas of the learning process. That of D.O. Hebb can be considered the most dependent upon physicalistic postulates. Yet Hebb took care to reduce the strength of his reliance on physiological data; as examples, these passages:

> Until neurological theory is much more adequate, the psychologist has to take it with a grain of salt . . . some aspects of behavior can never be dealt with in neurological terms alone . . . Psychology cannot become a branch of physiology. We cannot escape the need of

large-scale units of analysis, nor the need of the special methods of behavioral study on which such analysis is based.

Though we must get as much value from neurologizing as we can, it will never be possible to substitute neurology for Psychology. The complexity of the events controlling behavior is too great to be analyzed in terms of nerve impulses or the detailed relations between specific structures of the CNS (1958, pp. 262-265).

In the reinforcement behaviorism of Skinner, an obviously extremist anti-physiological bias can be seen as a foundation-stone. One of the theorist's autobiographical declarations includes an account of the history of this dogma in personal terms; writing of the formative years at Harvard, Skinner revealed:

I soon came into contact with W.J. Crozier, who had studied under Loeb. It had been said of Loeb . . . that he 'resented the nervous system.' Whether this was true or not, the fact was that both these men talked about animal behavior without mentioning the nervous system and with surprising success. So far as I was concerned, they cancelled out the physiological theorizing of Pavlov and Sherrington and thus clarified what remained of the work of these men as the beginnings of an independent science of behavior. (1956, p. 223)

No theorist has been more loyal to his training than Skinner in his insistence that the psychologist can do without neurologizing.

The best reasons for insisting that Psychology and physiology remain separate and apply their instruments of measurement to unlike phenomena are not practical but logical. A science is perpetually redefined by the data it finds and the sense it makes of them. Yet, at every stage of this renewal process, there are occasions for *a priori* judgments to be made which determine an emerging course the science will take. These constitute decisions; no matter how they are founded on expediency they require something more—a kind of daring. Surely if, in outer space, an animal is discovered to exist, capable of flight but in all other respects to be constructed as a fish-like organism, it will be left to the determination of ornithologists to take up its study or not. The history of ornithology records many such instances of choice that are reducible to exercises in the logic of language.

Then for Psychology to remove from its domain all physiological explanations is solely justified by the choice to have one category of scientific explanation that is not a physiological explanation. To reject all data found by physiologists or stated in the terms of physiologists is a decision calculated to imply that there are psychologists. The human organism is a physiological machine. This the psychologist chooses to ignore. In turn, the physiologist ignores the fact that the human organism is a slowly-moving mass composed of rapidly-moving sub-atomic particles. To the scientist whose subject is a galaxy, the human organism can not be proven to exist at all.

If rejecting by fiat the necessity of physiological explanations of learning took behaviorist Psychology more than forty years to accomplish, other decisions were more swiftly to be acknowledged by agreement. The later Wundt has been cited as having denied that Psychology was aptly called a "science of mind"; the effort of Watson to bring Psychology up to the status of a strict empirical science has been traced. One by one, the mind, "psyche," and consciousness were removed as subjects of psychologists' observations. And this occurred not under the justification that these subjects were not to be considered as within the province of this special science. Rather, it was concluded that, as scientific subjects, they did not matter.

Once the decision to relinquish thoughts as subject had been made in order to raise introspective philosophizing to the level of an objective science and to get on to the concept of the response, there was no returning of Psychology to psyche. In reality, there was no returning of the science to the insides of organisms. There are cognitive, psychoanalytical, and field psychologies. Yet these are all compromise doctrines; in a sense, they each imply and rely on mediational hypotheses. To say that something occurs between stimulus reception and response emission is to be perfectly justified as a theorist. Nevertheless, the status of intervening-variable theories is questionable in any science; they seldom contain more than "holding" concepts; they catch the fancy and suspend the attention until more efficient solutions will be produced. For instance, no latter-day Tolmanian would deny that "sign-gestalt expectancies" must be shown to be tangibly real to be incorporated meaningfully into any learning theory of the future; there is only one possible reply: that a physiologist will yet reveal their true representation in cortical transmission. If that were to take place, Tolman's name for it would not have been applied. Psychology withdrew from inside the organism for the final time.

One additional source of data was rejected by the behaviorist revolution. In the process of self-definition by which Psychology found its modern subject at the expense of its more traditional subjects, the product of other agonies of choice eliminated instincts. On the surface, this decision may be seen as a corollary to the retreat from physiological data, as well as a narrowing of the limits of those intra-organismic events which are to be admitted to psychological theory.

Psychology accepts for its theory no possibility that the behavior of organisms is regulated by genetic determinants. First, an hereditary causal explanation implies a specific temporal postulate; namely, that what is constitutional is fixed at conception; in other words, that whatever is to be imposed upon the organism by the union of egg cell and sperm cell will not be altered by conditions affecting the new organism in its development and will remain as the chromosome structure of that organism until death. The necessity of this postulate is ensured by the fact that—so far as is now known—the chromosomes are not modified by those post-conceptional events which in other ways modify the cells themselves. One may have, that is, skin darkened to the color of coffee by wind and sun, yet each cell of the body contains the Caucasian chromosome. This condition never changes. It is this absolute, inalterable genetic determination that first prevents its inclusion in psychological theory. For if behavior is determined by constitution alone, the problem of behavioral change is self-contradictory. Psychology takes as its prime subject *alteration* in the status of the organism; this it considers to be more important than whatever stability the organism itself might possess. The intention to explain learning thus precludes any acceptance of the genetic hypothesis.

Explanations of human behavior based on the hypothesis of instinctual cause have little place in modern Psychology. Hilgard's *Introduction to Psychology* makes this curtly clear to the novice by stating that "the concept of instinct has not proved helpful in studying or understanding human behavior." (1957, p. 121) Skinner's rejection of the hypothesis was more explicit:

> When we find, or think we have found, that conspicuous physical features explain part of man's behavior, it is tempting to suppose that inconspicuous features explain other parts. This is implied in the assertion that a man shows certain behavior because he was 'born that way.' To object to this is not to argue that behavior is never determined by hereditary factors. Behavior requires a behaving organism which is the product of a genetic process . . . But the doctrine of 'being born that way' has little to do with demonstrated facts. It is usually an appeal to ignorance. 'Heredity,' as the layman uses the term, is a fictional explanation of the behavior attributed to it. (1953, p. 26)

In this formulation, genetic determinism of human behavior was dismissed beyond recall. On its terms, all that heredity provides is an organism capable of acting in some way. Summarizing, Psychology is a science of behavior, the principal question it asks of nature being: how does behavior change? For this purpose, the new, post-revolutionary Psychology would seek to find laws of:

1. human behavior, especially human learning;
2. the causes of behavior apart from physical causes;
3. the causes of behavior apart from mental causes;
4. the causes of behavior apart from genetic causes.

When Psychology made its transformation from science of mental acts to science of physical acts, it moved closer to *process* and further from events as fixed, consistent entities. In the beginning, the overwhelming experimental problem was to isolate a response event under laboratory conditions of control. To accomplish this, the early behaviorists had need of an organism which performed crudely, overtly; they brought cats, dogs, white rats into laboratories. By this ingenuity, psychologists were able to isolate and objectify the response. It was only because of rigorous experimental methods applied to animals that Psychology reached its conceptual equivalent to the concepts molecule and atom. By observation of the simplicity of animal behavior, this science came upon its ultimate datum.

Yet there was a dilemma at the core of this empirical victory. The behavior of animals—while superbly quantifiable—remained elusive. It changed. Take the experience of Thorndike, the first behaviorist. Thorndike sought to observe what an animal does; he concentrated his attention upon its behavior. He watched a cat confined in a box escape from the box. Had he concluded his experiment then and there, Thorndike would have obtained these data: repeated trials—characterized by X, Y, etc.—lead to a response which solves the problem. If that had been the end of the experiment, the investigator would have provided certain information about a discrete response in the cat. Psychology would have known more about feline latch-opening.

Thorndike placed the animal in the box a second time, then again, and so forth. This decision brought Psychology nearer the ultimate subject of learning. The fruit of his persistence was that Thorndike found a progressive reduction in trial-and-error responding to precede the escape-producing response; this occurred as a function of successive experiences of the same cat in the same box, food reward outside the box, etc. In the attempt to narrow the subject of psychological observation to measurable dimensions, the observant behaviorist had encountered learning.

Thorndike's first monograph was on the subject of "animal intelligence"—what an animal can do. It was later—fifteen years later—that Thorndike was to write a "Psychology of learning," as one volume of his masterwork *Educational Psychology*. So this prolific originator may be said to have introduced to Psychology the task of explaining educational events. He had found that animals were educable—that even the least complex response can be seen within a process of behavioral change. It is less important that animal Psychology gained great impetus from Thorndike's work than that learning became a psychological subject.

In discussing certain basic requirements for a psychological theory of learning, it was presumed that the subject of learning is one to which Psychology turned in the course of its development from science of mind to science of behavior. In his review of the history of the behaviorist movement, Hebb concluded that "the only connected, consistent attempts at explanation in Psychology are to be found in one form or other of learning theory." (1960, p. 738) It is equally true that not much of practical value remains from the early years of behavioral experimentation in search of the secrets of learning. The sad fact was sadly recorded by Deese:

> At the beginning of the twentieth century there was much hope that the experimental study of learning would lead, in a fairly short time, to a scientific analysis of the problems of school and teaching. Many early books on learning were greatly concerned with the application of existing facts to problems of education . . . All in all, however, the experimental study of learning did not live up to the early hopes for application that it aroused. By 1930, workers in the field disclaimed any attempt to achieve results which would have educational significance . . . Theories of learning contained so little of interest to educators that such theories were relegated to an extremely minor role in the psychology of education. Since theories of learning had little or nothing of practical value to contribute, their place in textbooks was taken by new material on personality development, mental hygiene, etc. (1958, p. 327)

Yet a theory of learning has more recently made claims to be taken seriously as a contribution to practical problems of education. This claim will be tested later through an analysis of its central concepts.

II. CONDITIONING

Watson's behaviorism was not constructed as a learning psychology, no more than Thorndike's—in the beginning—had been intended as such. Both were environmentalists who strove to put down the genetic hypothesis once and for all. More than that, they were scientists. They gave to their science the quality of tough-minded devotion to empiricism that made the revolution stick and conferred a special character upon their own psychological systems.

One suspects that Pavlov the physiologist was a person of different temperament from these men. There is no denying that he was a rigorous scientist. Pavlov was a master surgeon. His dogs had had their jaws cut so that tubes leading from the salivary glands could bring the liquid out for collection. In that laboratory, someone turned on a metronome; it was noticed that salivary secretions could be brought under the control of that metronome and other stimulus events in the experimental setting. It is possible to imagine why it was that Pavlov did not see this magnificent accident as the extraordinary occasion of an organism learning. Pavlov knew all there was to know about dogs and most of what there is to know about salivation; he knew reflexes and functions of the brain. The fact that a dog had formed a relationship between a sound and its glands must not have seemed to Pavlov to have anything whatever to do with animal intelligence. It must have occurred to him that this mystifying phenomenon gave even less evidence of providing a solution to the problem of learning. That problem was not his concern in any case.

The word "conditioning" was chosen to refer to the result of that striking incident in 1927 in the laboratory at St. Petersburg. That is, the fact that a reflex had changed. A well understood stimulus-response pattern had been shown to be modifiable in a manner never previously suspected. This was not an instance in which a dog had learned to ride a bicycle by practice late at night when no one was looking. It was an instance in which what was assumed to have been a natural innate reaction pattern had got in some way confounded with totally irrelevant environmental circumstances. It was obvious that the new reaction pattern had once been unlearned—non-existent. Yet the auspicious chance occasion by which it entered the repertoire of the dog was not considered as a learned event. An entirely separate terminology had to be applied to express the fortuitous significance of what had happened inexplicably and at random.

There was admirable good sense in what has seemed to many an arbitrary Slavonic choice of word and, to others, a defect of translation. "Conditioning" expressed this surplus meaning: the phenomenon observed presents questions not of this order: what happened to the dog?; but rather, of this order: what did the metronome do? Thus without being at all aware of it, the men of the laboratory in St. Petersburg had discovered a new psychology of behavior. What Pavlov and his fellow theorists were convinced they had discovered were causal events taking place in brains—not stimuli but excitations irradiating across a cortex. The irony was complete.

Conditioning as subject began, in the first conditioning demonstration, with the simple, forceful, given fact that environmental events produce changes in responses. It progressed by steps such as these questions imply:

1. to what can the organism become conditioned?;
2. how does the environment condition the organism?

This revision in approach puts the principal focus of observation at a point no longer at the periphery of the organism but now totally at a point outside the organism. The environment was seen as containing events which were of the kind that could transform the organism in respect to its behavior. That is, Psychology took on the empirical problem of training—teaching.

The psychological study of conditioning has resulted in the discovery of more than one class of events considered to regulate behavioral change. Three major classes are expressed in various theories by means of: (1) the concept of the stimulus; (2) the concept of motive; and (3) the concept of the reinforcing stimulus. The premise by which each will be discussed is that they severally pertain to active events or processes that are, in themselves, sufficient to bring about changing behavior. On these terms, the three are distinct and need not interact one with the other to be causal.

The concept of the stimulus is not complex; it is a result of many years of intensive research contributed by the associationistic and sensationistic psychologies. The stimulus is conceived of as prior, extra-organismic, and causal. It may be defined as variable quanta of energy impinging upon a receptor organ; or, simply, as a change in the environment of a percipient organism. The definition is circular yet informative. It is circular in that the energy change in question is discovered by means of an observation of behavior on the part of the organism said to be stimulated. It informs that behavior exists in relationship with the environment. That is, behavior waits upon the environment to be caused. Behavior does not occur for no reason at all, is not accidental. It does not occur as a function of itself—responding-to-respond; it is not self-perpetuating. Nor does behavior necessarily occur as a function of events internal to the organism. This excludes from consideration the concept of proprioceptive stimulation; feedback stimuli from internal organs are conceptualized as causal in several theories which are not under consideration here. This discussion will stick to the limited but more direct and definitive conception of stimulus causes as external, as messages sent by the environment.

Motive has been infused with other properties in the relatively short time that motivation has been addressed as a psychological subject. Thus, by means of added postulates such as those referring to *learned* or *secondary motives*, the concept has been furnished with attributes that would make it more apt for explaining phenomena of human as opposed to infra-human behavior. In general, the concept of motivation as an internal organismic driving mechanism or fuel-supply for behavior has provided a sanctuary for mentalisms that have held superficial appeal. Such mentalistic constituents of the motive as will, reason, purpose, set, attention, etc. are in one form or another expressed as human motivational forces. It is easily seen that the trend is reactionary to the contributions of behaviorism; it has no place in the present discussion.

Specific theories of conditioning will be reviewed and criticized in the pages to follow. They are selected to demonstrate continuity in a progression that encompasses the brief history of behaviorial science. Each can be reduced to a descriptive paradigm summarizing its basic conceptual structure or its key postulates. In the designs for conditioning to be analyzed, five variables will constitute these basic terms; the variables are arranged in several combinations by the several theories; the variables are:

1. stimulus or stimuli—indicated by the symbol St;
2. organismic variable—O;
3. response—R;
4. goal object—G;
5. reinforcing stimulus—REIN.

Of these, only the organismic variable requires clarification. Several concepts of internal organismic causes have postulates concerning motivational influences upon behavior. As used in the analyses below, the organismic variable will include the full range of these collected concepts i.e.: (1) needs or metabolic processes; (2) neurological processes; (3) "thoughts" and other mentalistic entities; (4) mediational events and other mentalistic entities such as "percepts" and the rest of the family of inward experiences. For the most part, the organismic variable usually referred to will be of the kind typified by concepts of physiological needs or drives. The differing meanings, in this context, of goal and reinforcement will be explained as these concepts are introduced. The theories to be discussed are presented in roughly chronological order of their historical development and moments of strongest influence.

Connectionism

It has been argued that the chief pre-occupation of the founders of behaviorism was with experimental rigor. Their methodological reforms amounted to forceful reminders to psychologists to ignore all variables that were not measurable events. This preference for science took Thorndike—the later behaviorists following like trained cats—to the periphery of organisms and to the response. The end-product of whatever system would or could emerge was, *ipso facto*, behavior.

To find causal events for the peripheral behavioral events chosen for psychological explanations, Thorndike returned to stimuli as sensed. Thus external, sensory causes were considered to affect behavioral events. Thorndike's causes were very similar to those of Locke and Berkeley and Hume. Conncetionism became a theory of St→R relationships. In addition, a dynamic causal connection was said to exist between certain stimulus and response events. The paradigm in full can be shown graphically by this form.

Figure 1.

St $\xrightarrow{\text{WM}}$ R; (The symbol ⌐ ⌐ indicates a bond or connection and WM its dynamic properties.)

The bond or connection was built up among stimuli and responses by means of such factors as readiness, repetition, etc.. This is the basic connectionist paradigm; it is described without reference to the place within the general theory occupied by the law of effect, which is later to be discussed in detail with respect to the principle of reinforcement.

The theory of connectionism showed that stimuli and responses become connected under certain circumstances. It did not provide definitive information about how this happens—give substance to the connection itself. In this case, theory had far outrun data. In a sense it may be said that most of the psychological systems of this century have been dedicated to the solution of the puzzle left behind by connectionism. Physiological psychologists and cognitive psychologists have sought very different answers to the question of what links environmental with behavioral events. From this, it can be seen that connectionism as a theory was prototypic—an unfinished guide to the stimulus-response psychologies it inaugurated.

In summary, this theory proposed a bond or link between stimuli and responses. The nature of the bond itself was not specified. Behavioral events were considered as functions of stimulus events—related by means of functional or concomitant variation. The concept of the response was introduced as the target of psychological explanations and laws.

Purposivism

The full impact of Watson's methodological revolt was expressed in the "purposive behaviorism" proposed by Tolman. His was an objective Psychology based upon the results of animal experimentation. Yet Tolman reached much further into the future: he made an attempt at bridging the gulf of ideology which had separated animalistic from humanistic Psychology and threatened to grown more severe. A student of Holt, Tolman called his approach to conditioning a "molar" one—one which considered behavior as more than responses in their separate occurrences. Tolman had the notion that there is behavior plus something else; that something else is what behavior is "done for"; by this is meant that every instance of behavior presupposes its own purpose or goal.

It was the intention of Tolman to restore to Psychology a measure of its lost claim to respectability. If the early behaviorists had accomplished a rapprochement of this science with the standards of other sciences, it may have been that—in bringing animals into laboratories—it had sacrificed too much to this move forward. If it seemed reasonable to decide that only an exact, rigidly quantified science could be expected someday to be precise about behavior, it soon became obvious that psychologists might possibly get stuck at the lower orders of the phylogenetic scale. Tolman's solution was not to lead the rats out of the halls of science, but to establish a novel excuse for keeping them there. As Boring described this rationale in retrospect, it amounted to the fact that "Tolman . . . had saved purposiveness for rats, but he had kept true to behaviorism and had not given them back consciousness." (1957, p. 647) It is possible to infer from this description of Tolman's reasoning that, if infrahuman behavior could be shown to possess qualities of directedness or orientation to a goal, then these characteristics would be found present at maximum strength when the behavior of humans was eventually to become the subject of observation.

There were two principal descriptive concepts on which was founded purposive behaviorism. The paradigm can be summarized as:

Figure 2.

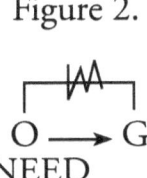

$$O \longrightarrow G$$
NEED

Written in this way, the model refers to a dynamic relationship established between tissue needs and goal objects. The concept is one by which certain events taking place within the organism are said to lead to movement of the organism in the direction of that object which will satisfy those needs. In this way, a link is conceptualized between need and a thing in the environment capable of restoring quiescence. This is a thoroughgoing concept in motivation; as such, it is the first to be considered by this review of theories; its counterparts will be found in several of the theories to be analyzed.

The purposivistic theory implies solely that:

1. the organism is driven;
2. the organism moves in the direction of goals;
3. the organism draws near to goals.

In summary, the concepts of Tolman's behaviorism have been examined. On the terms of the theory as examined, one can conclude that acts are performed (1) in relation to goals, or (2) as a function of organismic need-states. In fact, the most important contribution of purposive behaviorism was its tacit incorporation of the law of effect (See below.).

Omnibus Theory

This analysis of conditioning is about theories in general and not any single theory. Therefore, Hullian theory is included in the present discussion because it takes part in a progression of theoretical development; it leads to more recent formulations of the movement begun by the behaviorist revolution.

The ties joining purposivism and Hull's omnibus theory were stronger than was apparent during the long years of warfare between the Yaleman and Tolman, the Californian. Hull's system was more complex than those from which its several elements were derived; therefore the theory is given a name suggesting its characteristics as a collection or amalgam. In this sense, Hull brought one line traceable to the first efforts at behavioristic theory-making to a logical close. He made use of the complete range of available conceptual elements from which former theorists had selected only a sampling. In its intention to be summative, the Hullian system turned out to be no other than accumulative.

The concise paradigm of omnibus theory contains four elements—when its many limbs and branches are cut away to reveal its essential form. These first principles and their combination in an equation meant to explain conditioning can be shown graphically as follows:

Figure 3.

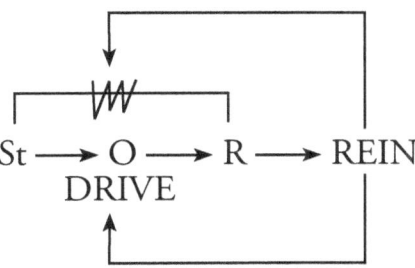

Note that Hull's theory can be placed in the general classification of those having *reinforcement* as a central explanatory concept. The difference is the addition of a specific organismic variable in a position intervening between conceptualized prior stimuli and responses. This formulation indicates that Hullian theory bears an unmistakable resemblance, in one respect, to those purposivistic concepts proposed to explain conditioning.

The theory of Hull took cognizance of the fact that organisms act in relation to sensed or imagined goal-objects—the organism moves toward goals. This aspect of behavior as "purposive" can naturally be assumed to have its origin in the fact that the organism exists in a state of tissue needs. That is, it is driven. A reinforcing object or stimulus was considered to possess dual properties. The model presented shows that, while reinforcement is restoring states of drive to equilibrium, it is at the same time having a particular effect upon stimulus-response relationships.

Hullian theory compels attention by virtue of its thoroughness. No controversial conception of how conditioning takes place was left out by Hull. The fact is that omnibus theory died a lengthy death of overuse. In the years before 1955, countless precise psychological investigations were set out to test specific postulates of Hull's theory. With respect to applications of the theory to human behavior, the Iowa school was well-equipped to carry out this ritual. The conditioning of blinks of the eyelid was scrutinized from every possible point of view—from that of drive propensities to that of ego-involvement. What the testers of Hullian constructs found would fill volumes.

Empirical investigations have proven that Hull produced a well-integrated, architecturally sound system of conditioning. Yet there are few practical situations involving the conditioning of human behavior for which the theory contributes to understanding. It may be that one cannot base an explanation of the causes of human learning on any principle derived from omnibus theory alone—that is, not taken over from antecedent theories it has merged. *Essentials of Behavior,* as well as *Principles of Behavior,* are not texts for teachers, nor did any other of Hull's written work present practical descriptions of how conditioning is done.

Hullian theory has been called omnibus for the reason that it synthesized the complete set of elements found in the several theories chosen for this review. That is, it contained an hypothesized organismic variable—of the need or drive category—both stimulus and response variables, the concept of a dynamic or functional bond joining stimuli with responses, and a goal-attainment variable possessing reinforcing properties—capable of exerting causal force upon the functional bond. Hull's theory can be considered comprehensive of most explanatory systems of conditioning prior to his own.

The Hullian omnibus system did not fall by experimental disproof or logical refutation. To the extent that most critics consigned it to the status of a noble failure, the theory was only accused of falling under its own weight. The following summation of Hilgard's was, of all criticisms, perhaps the most fair:

> It must be acknowledged that Hull's system, for its time, was the best there was—not necessarily the one nearest to psychological reality, not necessarily the one whose generalizations were most likely to endure—but the one worked out in the greatest detail . . . Furthermore, it may well be said to have been the most influential of theories between 1930 and 1950, judging from the experimental and theoretical studies engendered by it . . . Its primary contribution may turn out to lie not in its substance at all, but rather in the ideal it set for a genuinely systematic and quantitative psychological system . . . (1956, p. 182)

It is important that Hull was a thoroughgoing behaviorist, and that the concept of the reinforcing stimulus was the force which made his system go. Apart from maintaining the established traditions of twentieth-century Psychology, Hull added to the experience of the science one unintended gift. This was a newly-discovered awareness of the *limits* to which theory-building in Psychology can be extended. Omnibus theory accumulated explanatory concepts of conditioning; from its fall, it became necessary for psychological theorists to reduce their theories of conditioning in complexity. Only a theory simpler than Hull's could supplant its undoubted claim to influence. A system of conditioning succeeding to omnibus theory would have to contain fewer than the 178 theorems and corollary propositions Hull left to his science. Such a theory would require fewer component parts. A theory meeting this requirement will be analyzed in chapters of this book to follow.

The three conditioning paradigms presented in brief review can be seen in perspective by observation of their contrasting central explanatory principles. These are:

1. connectionism: given a stimulus, then a response;
2. purposivism: given a need, then arrival at a goal;
3. omnibus theory: given a reinforcing stimulus, then a stronger habit.

This commentary serves no more than an organizing function. It is oversimplified to the point at which each theory is so compressed that it is scarcely recognizable. Yet a definite progression from simple to complex can be observed. In addition, it becomes clear that—as theories of conditioning have evolved—the operative principle around which newly emerging theories has been constructed is that of reinforcement. Thus while behavioral change was once considered to depend upon prior stimulus conditions, it is now considered to depend upon *post-response* stimulus conditions.

III. REINFORCEMENT

The concept of conditioning has been considered to refer to events causal of the learning of organisms. This means that conditioning events initiate patterns of behavioral change. Conditioning agents impose upon the organism a process of variability in behavior. To behave is to change from one response to another.

The development of Hullian omnibus theory brought the art of theorizing in Psychology to a point of no return. After Hull, theorists became constrained to reduce the complexity of his explanatory system—to eliminate from his model of behavioral change one or more terms, to simplify his equation. In the following chapter, an examination will be made of a specific theory of conditioning that has accomplished this demanding objective.

For the student of the history of behaviorism as a movement holding immeasurable influence upon theory-building in modern Psychology, it will come as no surprise to know that organismic variables could not survive as key events to explain how conditioning works. For all his apparent intentions to remake psychological research in accord with the methods of physiology, Watson was never a physiologist. The nominal founder of behaviorism did not propose a psychology to be expressed in the language of physiological data. Watson contributed to Psychology its modern methods of approach to problems that were traditionally psychological; he insisted that Psychology look at organisms as behaving mechanisms rather than as ghost-inhabited machines. If there was thought, it was for Watson expressed in the movement of muscles—not by glands or neural discharges or metabolic states.

The first published paper by Skinner was a clarification of the concept of the reflex. In *Behavior of Organisms*, the first fully developed theoretical distinction between two kinds of conditioning was proposed. They are, succinctly: conditioning of the Pavlovian or "classical" kind; conditioning of the operant or "instrumental" kind. Operant theory is to be analyzed in minute detail in this and a subsequent chapter. It is important first to state what made it possible. That is, how it came to be discovered.

By experimenting with a white rat in a specially-devised apparatus resembling a box, Skinner found that the rat could become conditioned to depress a small metal bar protruding from one wall of the structure. A change took place in the behavior of the animal: the frequency or rate of its pressing of the bar increased. This occurred in the case of more than one rat introduced one at a time in the apparatus; a phenomenon had been established. Responses were replaced—in the Skinner box—by others which occurred more rapidly in time in relation to each-other. The task of Skinner as investigator of this phenomenon was to find out what had caused the change.

It was realized that, in any situation in which the conditioning of an organism happens, the environment of that organism is at no time still. The environment can be described as an ever-moving field of events. It produces stimuli without ceasing; some of these are above-threshold for the organism. In this "blooming, buzzing confusion," William James' famous metaphor, the organism is considered to be immersed in quantities of potentially stimulating events and processes of the surround.

For the operant conditioner, this observation reduces to absurdity such questions as: what stimulus caused that response?; what stimulus caused that response to increase in strength? At this point in the study of conditioning, Skinner had arrived at his own answers. By framing the problem in another context, he had created the problem anew.

Skinner asked: does the initial stimulus have to be found? It will be obvious that this crucial rearrangement of the problem was an artifact of an experimental situation. A box had been designed for use in finding out about animal learning; in this device, there were myriad possible stimulus objects and myriad possible properties of these objects—for example, the color and light-reflecting properties of the metal walls, the shape and dimensions of the box and bar, atmospheric conditions, etc.. Further, around the box innumerable events were taking place—for example, noises occurring in the laboratory, changes in temperature of the room, smells and sights of psychologists coming and going and peering into the box, etc.. The experimental situation itself lacked rigid internal controls; it refused to remain at rest.

Operant theory stands upon a methodological discovery. It was found that one does not have to vary, directly, prior stimulus conditions as independent variables in order to bring about the conditioning of a white rat to press a bar in a Skinner box. That is, one does not have to isolate, identify, or categorize prior stimuli present in or around the box; the animal will come to press the bar even if the experimenter has no information concerning which of these stimuli caused that to happen.

Perhaps because of the type of apparatus designed by Skinner to study conditioning, the prior stimulus disappeared. For whatever ultimate reason the operant conditioning paradigm came to be developed, it is important that behavioral events are by this theory considered to be "emitted" and not "elicited"; this means that they are *found* to occur; their causes are not specified in terms of prior stimulus events in the traditional sense. This is the conceptual breakthrough achieved by operant theory and to which its concepts are grounded. This defines the departure from conditioning of the "classical" sort to conditioning of the "instrumental" variety.

The causes of behavioral change proposed as explanations by operant theory will be analyzed below. For preliminary discussion, it is assumed that the concept of the operant response took psychological theorizing to a point of extreme simplification. With the first behaviorists, Skinner had eliminated organismic variables from his explanatory system. His system transcended *their* formulations by eliminating the concept of the prior stimulus. This new formula contributed the manifest virtue of brevity. Its essential form is: $R \rightarrow St$. It changed significantly the position of the stimulus. Operant theory suggested that behavior change occurs as a function of those stimulus events which behavior *produces*.

To recapitulate, operant theory reversed the position of stimulus variables in its solution to the problem of how behavioral change occurs. It took the key causal variable and placed it *after* behavior. From this point in psychological theorizing, the concept of St→R became an anachronism; the former stimulus-response theories of behavior had been supplanted. Psychologists were counseled to abandon the search for the eliciting stimulus.

Operant conditioning theory is the dominant explanatory system of modern Psychology. In its complete form, it can be described by this paradigm:

Figure 4.

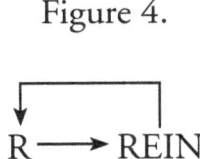

By this formulation, it is apparent that the determining, subsequent stimulus event is expressed in a new/old language. The concept of reinforcement is proposed to explain the *effects* of responding upon response. The prior stimulus has disappeared from the explanatory model. Nothing takes its place. Therefore, reinforcement has its effect upon response alone. With the operant model, the terminology of conditioning theory became markedly more simple. Now it is possible to propose that reinforcement affects the strengths of responses. It was formerly necessary to state that reinforcement strengthens *relationships* formed by stimulus events and response events. This conjunctive or correlative property, to which theorists once referred as the establishing of an environmental-organismic bond, is now avoided. Thus it is superfluous or wrong to postulate: first the bond, then the stronger or weaker bond. In the revised formulation: first response, then the stronger or weaker response. The prior stimulus—because it is prior—once was assumed to be predominant among the several events occurring in the mechanism. It was possible to say that the organism waits upon prior stimuli. Under terms of operant theory, reinforcement—although subsequent—assumes predominance.

An evaluation of the concept of reinforcement, its explanatory value and significance for an understanding of how conditioning works, depends on analysis of the propositions of operant theory. It may be said that the full impact of the law of effect upon Psychology was not recognized until the concept of reinforcement had replaced the law itself. There was no thoroughgoing theory of reinforcement in Psychology until the operant paradigm had been presented and assimilated. Thus logical problems intrinsic to both law of effect and reinforcement were left untended, submerged, their solutions deferred. Only now must psychologists come to grips with the concept of reinforcement expressed in its complete and most forceful form by operant theory.

Differences between the classical and operant or instrumental explanations of conditioning take the following major forms:

1. smooth-muscle and glandular conditioning is explained by classical theory; striped-muscle conditioning is explained by operant theory;
2. in general, the conditioning of involuntary responses can be described as classical, while operant conditioning is of voluntary responses.

Uniquely among psychological theorists, Skinner opposed the construction of theories in Psychology. Thus, in order to seem to be an honest critic of theory-making, he has had to seem not to have produced anything meeting the terms of his own definition of what a theory is or could be. His article "Are Theories of Learning Necessary?" appeared in 1950. For a time thereafter, the question of whether Skinner would be allowed to take credit on both sides of the argument had a certain vogue for writers whose subject was Psychology as a science. It was a paradox which weighed heavily on Verplanck, who wrote:

> In dealing with Skinner, we are concerned with a theorist who now espouses no theory, a systematist whose system is still developing, and a constructive thinker some of whose most important contributions have been those of a critic. (1954, p. 268)

Yet on the same page, Verplanck took note of the fact that

> Skinner sees as the problem of modern Psychology the development of a comprehensive system, or theory of behavior ... (1954, p. 268)

Published in 1938, *The Behavior of Organisms* was Skinner's first book; it was patently theoretical. It contained—in its introductory chapter—a list of twenty-four "laws of learning"; these were not propositions stating laws of nature; they were definitional concepts. As Verplanck put it,

> [Operant conditioning] is a highly formal, but not highly formalized, theory ... Rather than being

a set of empirical laws embodying statements
that represent inductive generalizations based
on a set of terms initially defined in a data
language, it is a set of formally defined terms,
and defining laws, which are only coordinated
with data-language statements after they have
been fully stated, (1954, p. 295)

No one doubts that Skinner—despite his professed
aversion to theory construction in Psychology—once
presented to his colleagues a set of at least tentative
theoretical hypotheses. In 1954, Verplanck was not sure;
his critical article continued as follows:

Skinner . . . is preoccupied with the problem of
arriving at empirical laws, by induction, from
data. He explicitly rejects theory construction
by the axiomatic method . . .

In developing a system, Skinner has, however,
inadvertently written a theory and has
formulated as empirical law statements of the
sort that serve as the postulates of a system.
(1954, pp 300, 301).

The facts of the case are the following:

1. the 1938 version of operant theory presented
   numerous deductive concepts; some of these have
   been cited by this discussion;
2. just before or during the writing of *Science and
   Human Behavior*, which appeared in 1953,
   Skinner began to question the feasibility of
   further elaboration of theory in Psychology; his

anti-theoretical paper had suggested that, for the time being, attempts at the formulation of comprehensive systems of behavior be suspended;

3. in *Science and Human Behavior*, the tone taken by the theorist was less grand and more practical; the twenty-four "laws" were not stated as such; rather, they were translated into maxims or homilies set forth in the language of common sense.

At this point in the chronology, it could truthfully have been said that Skinner—once a theorist—had retired to a position of tough-minded empiricism. Opposed to dogma, he had adopted the patient, trial-and-error attitude of the experimentalist. Content to stay in the laboratory, he looked forward to the day when some breakthrough or discovery might permit Psychology another, wiser try at an all-encompassing conceptual scheme.

It will never be known what caused the former theorist to make this retreat into the laboratory. From postulating law-like generalities, Skinner turned to data collection. The transformation was effected in the next book in the operant conditioning series to emerge, *Schedules of Reinforcement* (1957), with Charles Ferster as co-author; this book was a compilation of results from several years of experimentation on animals, a detailed research report. Speculation on the reasons for this intensive empirical stage of the operant system may hold fascination for the historian of the Psychology of the nineteen-fifties. One line of argument might show that the need for explanation of how conditioning takes place was set aside by the growing tendency for the activities of operant laboratories to *produce* behavioral change instead of studying it. This refers to the announced intention of operant conditioners to impose *control* on the responses of rats and pigeons, to create orderly relationships among environmental and behavioral events. It refers to the attempt to produce—as in a factory—certain behaviors by the application of "techniques" within the laboratory setting. It represented a proposal to psychologists that they train animals.

The pre-occupation of operant psychologists with controlling began in earnest in the nineteen-fifties. This unique approach to the conduct of science was described by Skinner and his followers in a number of anecdotal and methodological books and papers (e.g.: Skinner, 1947, 1956, 1957, 1958, 1960; Sidman, 1960, Findley, 1962). One reason for this development is clear; the operant conditioning method of experimentation is one that permits conditioned responses (1) to be studied and (2) to be created.

With a feckless candor, operant conditioners have described their activities as if to control was a scientific discovery in its own right; these passages from Skinner's writings will serve as examples:

> I suddenly found myself face to face with the engineering problem of the animal trainer. When you have the responsibility of making absolutely sure that a given organism will engage in a given sort of behavior at a given time, you quickly grow impatient with theories of learning . . . Manipulation of environmental conditions alone made possible a wholly unexpected practical control. Behavior can be shaped up according to specifications and maintained indefinitely almost at will. (1956, p. 228)

The practical task before us created a new attitude toward the behavior of organisms. We had to maximize the probability that a given form of behavior would occur at a given time. We could not enjoy the luxury of observing one variable while allowing others to change in what we hoped was a random fashion. We had to discover all relevant variables and submit them to experimental control whenever possible . . . Our task forced us to emphasize prior experimental control, and its success in revealing orderly processes gave us an exciting glimpse of the superiority of laboratory practice over verbal explanation. (1960, p. 36)

These self-descriptive statements imply that certain psychologists had forgotten what scientific method is. By taking to an extreme the behaviorist lesson that psychological experiments should be conducted with more rigor, those who have put this dogma into practice have attempted to make rigorous their *dependent* variables.

Some amateur theorists among operant conditioners have gone further than proposing that their methods of controlling are preferable to the *investigation* of behavior in Psychology. That is, they have claimed more for their revised methodology than that it solves problems of psychological research. As signs of this trend, the following compendium of statements is provided:

Experimental control refers to our ability to manipulate behavior . . . (Sidman, 1960, p. 342)

The adequacy of a technique should be assessed in terms of the precision and reliability of the control it achieves . . . One of the criteria of a new technique is its success in producing data that have never been seen before. (Sidman, 1960, pp. 18, 22)

It is basically the experimenter's job to gain control over . . . environmental conditions. (Findley, 1962, p. 113)

. . . variations in behavior from one experimenter to another, or within a given experimenter, suggest that he can state definitive relationships between himself and his organism only insofar as he is able to control and manipulate the relevant environmental conditions . . .

The material to follow represents . . . the results of several years of laboratory effort in which the pursuit of behavioral control progressively took precedence over the statement of problems and answers, and in which it was often pursued in their absence.

The major result of this effort has been a demonstration that it is feasible to build, describe, and manipulate complex samples of behavior under controlled conditions . . . It has been the argument of this section that to do so is in many ways basic to the building of a science of behavior. (Findley, 1962, p. 113)

> Although frequently discussed under the guise of many theoretical and philosophical concepts, the problem of experimental control is basically one of 'how does the experimenter make the organism do what he desires?' . . . (Findley, 1962, p. 115)

These passages indicate that methods of controlling data are recommended to science in general—as a solution to problems of research faced by any scientist. It is certain that no scientist will pay attention to these proposals. In fact, the true scientist will find them incoherent.

The trends described here can only serve—if allowed to continue—to reduce the scientific stature of Psychology. If they are not to be reversed, they may not be ignored. It is crucial to determine what started them in the first place. In this sense, one must examine the behavior of psychologists. In the years following World War II, there was a proliferation of laboratories that were oriented to questions of how conditioning works, according to the instrumental as opposed to the classical interpretation. When, after a few years, Skinner himself had withdrawn support for any more sophisticated elaborations of his own theory based on new findings, those who were committed to the instrumental model were left with few explicit hypotheses to test by following the usual requirements of scientific method. Encouraged no longer to tests postulates of a theory which was not yet fully written—that seemed likely never to be written—operant conditioners found an opportunity to experiment, if such is possible, with methods of experimentation. In their work with rats, they relied on the Skinner box; they soon saw that, in this apparatus, some manipulation of the situation would insure that a hungry rat could be induced to press the bar, receive food, and begin the process which was the object of experimental concern. The technique devised, called "successive approximations," was an invention that swiftly brought the bar-pressing response under control. With this device, precise and impressive feats of animal training were demonstrable.

Operant conditioners became aware—in the course of conducting studies of conditioning—that the behavior of organisms is remarkably pliant and easily controlled. With the use of the principle of reinforcement for "correct" responses, these psychologists could produce intricate "chains" of behavior at will. From a contemporary report, one learns of the talented rat which,

> in a special experimental box, engaged in the following sequence of behavior: it climbed to the top of a spiral staircase, 'bowed to the audience,' pushed down a drawbridge, crossed the bridge, climbed a ladder, used a chain to pull in a model railroad car, pedaled the car through a tunnel, climbed a flight of stairs, ran through a tube, and stepped into an elevator which descended to the base of the platform (raising the school banner). At this point a buzzer sounded, and the rat pressed a lever and received a food pellet. (Kelleher and Gollub, 1962, p. 544)

This exercise in control is not startling when one considers that the history of controlling organisms is as old as man's history. In that sense, there have been "psychologists" whose major concern was conditioning for at least five thousand years. Yet the problem of why operant psychologists—turned away from continued *investigation* of this phenomenon and more important phenomena remains a puzzle. They, by their own admission, became fascinated with the phenomenon not for itself but for its immediate applications. This can only be attributed to the intense confidence felt by them in the infallible power of the method. They had stumbled onto a too-good thing.

There is a theory which can definitely be identified as "operant theory." In spite of his warnings to the contrary, Skinner's supporters have made efforts at theorizing. To a large extent they have been content to elaborate postulates of the theory which define the number and kinds of reinforcement variations there can be; this work is at least partly grounded in *a priori* speculations—that is, it presents hypotheses for testing. Further, Skinner himself was not idle as a theorist. His *Verbal Behavior*, which originated in lectures given in 1948 but did not appear in book form until 1957, represented an attempt to frame a system of operant concepts designed to explain *human* behavior.

According to operant theory, conditioning occurs as a function of the reinforcing stimuli *obtained from* the environment by responses. The law of effect is thus considered to be the prime law governing behavioral change. This restitution of Thorndike's principle at the core of this much more recent theory was acknowledged by Keller and Schoenfeld:

> When you compare the work of Skinner with that of Thorndike you may be impressed by the numerous dissimilarities. The two men used different species of animals, different apparatus,

and different experimental procedures. Yet,
when you consider that both situations required
a manipulation of some experimental object;
when you note the presentation of food was in
each case contingent upon this manipulation;
and when you compare the principle of Type
R [instrumental] conditioning with the law of
effect, you may notice a striking agreement.
Both formulations emphasize the influence of
the outcome of a response upon its strength:
Thorndike calls it [the outcome] 'satisfaction'
and Skinner speaks of a 'reinforcing stimulus.'
(1950, pp. 51, 52)

Here is a translation of terms from the language of one
theory to the language of another. The phrase " . . . the
influence of the outcome of a response upon its strength"
will be subjected to thorough analysis later on. For the
moment, the fact that the law of effect has not been totally
incorporated into operant theory requires discussion.
It is important to see just what the law implies to the
operant conditioner and, in addition, what concepts
have been grafted upon the law or set forth as corollaries
to it. This discussion will be focused upon: conditioned
reinforcement; positive reinforcement; and, partial
reinforcement.

Conditioned reinforcement

This is the principle of secondary reinforcement—by
which certain reinforcing stimuli said not to be originally
capable of "strengthening behavior" acquire capacities
that enable them to be considered capable of doing so.
This change in hypothesized properties of the stimulus

is said to occur as a function of stimulus generalization. That is, its presence in the environment of the organism when the organism is being positively reinforced may cause it to take on "value" equal to that of a primary reinforcing agent. Thus the process occurs by association of stimuli.

According to this concept, it is possible that an organism can become conditioned not only to make certain responses: it can become conditioned to certain reinforcements. Thus a token which is presented to a chimpanzee for some response can serve as a reinforcement for that response if the token has previously been replaced repeatedly by a sought-after piece of food. Under these conditions, the chimpanzee will perform the response in question simply to obtain tokens. When this occurs, tokens are considered to have become conditioned as reinforcements.

The empirical basis for the concept conditioned reinforcement is not questioned. The following discussion relates to its function in operant or any other reinforcement theory. The concept permits any stimulus present in the environment of the organism immediately subsequent to a given response to be called a reinforcing stimulus; this is said to be true only if there is observed some change in the organism's behavior. The concept will be seen to be of the definitional type. It expands the range of possible referents which are included by the term "reinforcement"; any thing or event can therefore be referred to by that term if a specific result is produced by that thing or event. This definitional postulate—as expanded—has as its most direct result a broadening in scope of the law of effect.

Using the principle of conditioned reinforcement, operant theory is far better equipped to claim significance for its description of the facts of learning than it would be without such a principle. The description becomes relevant to behavioral change which is not governed solely by the satisfaction of primary appetites. Thus it moves away from reliance on such preoccupations of purposivism as demands, disturbances, and quiescence. The theorist does not have to make measurements of or state propositions concerning prior tissue-needs or states of the organism. In that sense, operant theory is free to move forward in the direction of a firm anti-physicalist stand.

To recapitulate, the principle of conditioned reinforcement has been discussed both as a specific concept among those of operant theory and as a proposition having important implications for conditioning theory in general. In the first instance, conditioned reinforcement is a definitional principle; as is the case with most concepts within the reinforcement category, its definition refers to what it is in terms of what it does. In the second instance, conditioned reinforcement implies a new interpretation of the reinforcement principle by shifting the source of effect from inside the organism to the environment of the organism.

It is not surprising that the conditioned reinforcing agent has come to be described as the primary causal variable which regulates *human* as opposed to animal behavior. For it can be seen that—to whatever extent the operant system can be credited with explaining how human behavior changes—it must contain a postulate such as this one. No theory advanced to explain the effects of conditioning upon humans could be expected to rely solely on a principle of primary reinforcement. Human learning manifestly does not depend upon the satisfaction of gut hungers alone. To propose that it does would be to return to those theories that once put heavy emphasis on the causal influence of bodily humors and the turgidity of blood. The concept of conditioned reinforcement is a necessary component of those theories having the intention to encompass more than the conditioning of infrahuman organisms.

Positive reinforcement

This is a principle taken over without alteration from the later, revised version of the law of effect. As Thorndike left the law, it had been divided sharply into halves. On the basis of his own experimentation, Thorndike reluctantly concluded that punishment did not have the same effect to produce extinction that "reward" had to produce acquisition. Thus the law of effect had not been empirically supported as a neat polarity; the part having to do with conditioning had been verified, but alternative explanations were required for the phenomena of extinction.

The principle of positive reinforcement states that certain events which follow a response can have a strengthening effect upon the response. As confirmed by Skinner and other operant conditioners, this is the modern, approved version of Thorndike's law. The concept of punishment has been fully discredited as a factor capable of *reversing* the conditioning paradigm. As formulated by operant theory, the complete explanation of acquisition/extinction takes this form: positive reinforcement possesses greater power to condition a response than the power possessed by punishment to remove it. In this context, it is important to see in what way a positive reinforcement differs from a punishment. To refer by the former to objects such as food and water or events such as sexual release, and to refer by the latter to events such as an electric shock will serve to separate the meanings of the two terms for the present.

Implications of the concept of positive reinforcement are complex and extensive. The principle indicates, first of all, that behavior which is under the control of reinforcement is in large measure dependent upon such "goods" as the organism can derive by its means. It implies that a response is directed toward taking valued objects out of the behaver's environment. Secondly, the withdrawal of the concept of punishment from equivalent status to that of the reinforcement principle implies that responses are more readily conditioned than they are unconditioned. With regard to punishment, it is said that events of this class create effects which tend to *distract* the organism—human or animal—from concentration upon the learning situation; that is, from performing certain responses to the exclusion of others. Such events as frustration by a barrier or inflicted pain are, on these terms, conducive more to hesitancy to respond than to the orderly replacement of old behavior by new behavior that characterizes the course of learning.

The theory argues that when an organism responds "incorrectly" and is punished, the conditioning situation is not advanced or retarded but, rather, is distorted. This occurs because the "correct" response—one which may in future permit the organism to avoid punishing circumstances—does not become apparent to the organism. The organism "learns" only that it has responded incorrectly; therefore punishment serves to direct the organism, by an inescapable signal, to error. When punishing circumstances intervene upon a potential learning situation, the organism may not simply turn its attention to the causes of these punishing consequences;

instead, it may attend solely to the punishment itself—
its severity or duration. It may spend time licking its
wounds; the organism becomes frozen into stability in
the midst of an active environment. It is simply having a
pain or suffering an injury; it is merely being punished.
When this happens, the theory argues, error reduction
becomes an insurmountable task. In fact, it is precisely
those emotional psychomotor and autonomic responses
that commonly follow upon punishing circumstances
which alone can be conditioned in the situation.

The most straightforward effects of punishment upon
conditioning are considered by operant theory to be:

1. concentration upon error;
2. and, conditioned emotionality.

In fact, these results are conceptualized as having more
direct relevance to the unsuitability of punishment than
the general slowness and lack of effectiveness of punishing
events to bring about the unlearning of a response.
What is still left unanswered here is the question of how,
according to the theory, one can get rid of "incorrect"
behavior.

The reciprocal of the operant principle of positive
reinforcement is not punishment, nor what might be
called "negative" reinforcement. It is rather the *absence* of
reinforcement. Operant theory formulated the concept
of "withholding" reinforcement. This represents its
central principle for extinction of behavior. With this
concept, the two halves of the operant derivation of
the law of effect can be matched. The theory holds that
behavioral change occurs as a function of the production
of "goods" from the environment by means of those
responses which are being learned. By contrast, operant

theory holds that when the behavior of an organism fails to obtain positively reinforcing objects or events, the responses in question will be observed to *decrease* in strength. Should no further "good" be produced by a response, operant theory proposes that the response will continue to decline in frequency of occurrence; the fact that an unreinforced response may eventually reach zero frequency is attributed to its inability to obtain reinforcement of any kind. It leads to nothing. This is the operant explanation of how extinction occurs.

It can be seen that reinforcement can be equated with positive reinforcement. If there is no place in the conceptual structure of the system for punishment variables, it is only necessary to speak of the controlling propensities of rewarding events or the absence of such events. The theory focuses primary attention on the building-up of responses in the repertoire of the organism. It invests more concern with the causes of learning than with causes of, for example, forgetting or repression. Thus the theory moves in the direction of the following solution to the disappearance of behaviors from a repertoire: responses replace other responses.

To the operant theorist, responses are not necessarily lost; they can be pushed aside. This implies that it may be true—as common sense would have it—that it is an easier thing to condition a correct response following a mistaken one, than it is to eradicate that mistake first and then proceed to a correct response. If the operant formulation of positive reinforcement is one-sided, still it satisfies requirements of parsimony to which, since Lloyd Morgan, all psychological theories have had to pay tribute. Throughout the discussions to follow in this chapter and the next, the term "reinforcement" will be used as a shortened version of "positive reinforcement";

this is intended to refer to a class of events best described as "goods" or rewards.

Partial reinforcement

This concept has its empirical basis in research reported by Ferster and Skinner in *Schedules of Reinforcement* (1957). The concept may be stated as follows: greater control over learning can be obtained by occasional than by continuous reinforcement. This means that the power of reinforcement to condition behavioral change is optimal when certain responses of a class are reinforced but others are not. Thus when the environment manipulates both reinforcement and non-reinforcement through some kind of balanced procedure, it achieves best results in conditioning the organism.

This off/on conception of response-produced reinforcement stimuli has been demonstrated as apt for describing the conditioning of rats, chimpanzees, and pigeons. It is possible to increase the frequency of pigeon key-pecking responses to such rapidity that the human observer has difficulty in counting them—mechanical recorders must be used. This is done simply by providing reinforcements to a pigeon on an *intermittent* basis. In most cases of experiments of this type, the pattern of responses to be reinforced is planned beforehand and the food-delivering apparatus pre-set. This is what is referred to as the "scheduling" of reinforcing events.

It is at once clear that the phenomena of partial reinforcement cannot be incorporated into any thoroughgoing theory of reinforcement. If a reinforcing stimulus can be said to exert causal force upon conditioning, then its continuous use would be expected to have stronger effects than its occasional use.

It is true to say that operant theorists have seldom attempted to conceptualize their own irrefutable data with regard to partial reinforcement. This attempt is nowhere successfully carried out by any statement of the theory.

In coming to terms with the phenomena of partial reinforcement, no operant theorist has formulated the compromise position on reinforcement which these data make necessary. This source of contradiction was noted by Deese, who wrote:

> This . . . effect of partial reinforcement is of the greatest theoretical and practical importance. For one thing, it enables us to understand why behavior in natural settings is likely to be so persistent—most behavior is probably not reinforced for each try . . .
>
> Thus, inconsistency in the application of reinforcement is the stuff of which persistent behavior is made. How much an inconsistent application of reinforcements . . . is responsible for a generalized trait of persistence we do not know. (1958, pp. 67, 71)

In this case, it can be seen that the postulates of operant theory have not be revised to take account of schedules. To the extent that methods of *programmed teaching* may have derived from this theory, there is no representation of partial reinforcement among the techniques proposed for teaching by programs. By contrast, continuous reinforcement is applied in these methods without exception. Here is a discrepancy between data and the practical application of a theory. Yet the main deficiency is conceptual and not one of the technology of education.

It has been shown that facts of the operation of partial reinforcement upon conditioning are incompatible with a reinforcement principle taken at full strength. Either compromises are required by which each concept can be synthesized into one postulate, or the explanatory truth of each must be challenged on logical grounds. The central questions on this subject can be reduced to:

1. does conditioning occur when positive reinforce ment follows responses and extinction occur when non-reinforcement follows responses?;
2. or, does conditioning occur when both positive reinforcement and non-reinforcement alternately follow responses?

The concepts of positive and partial reinforcement are bound together into a single problem of this nature: how much reinforcing has the strongest effect upon behavioral change?

To summarize the preceding review of second-order postulates of operant theory, the principles of conditioned, partial, and positive reinforcement have been introduced. Conditioned reinforcement was described as a deductive postulate which permits explanations to be made of human learning by terms other than those used to explain infrahuman learning. Positive reinforcement was described as an empirically-derived postulate which can be equated with "reinforcement" because both signify a single event. Partial reinforcement is another empirical postulate; the facts on which it is based were shown to present serious difficulties for any theory relying upon a strong interpretation of the reinforcement principle.

It is necessary next to examine in more detail the precise form taken by all reinforcement theories of conditioning. In the pages to follow, the structure of the reinforcement paradigm will be analyzed; it is important to see just what logical status that structure holds. So that this examination can rest upon firm ground, a clear presentation of the terminology and meaning of the law of effect must first be made, aided by the following passage from the writings of Spence:

> [In] simple . . . learning situations the psychologist has observed that when certain types of environmental events accompany or follow a particular response, the response is more likely to occur on subsequent occasions. (1956, p. 32)

What is described is the "empirical law of effect" as it has been defined in most texts. As Spence continued, this law

> . . . summarizes an observed relationship between the subsequent strength or likelihood of occurrence of a response and . . . different classes of effects or outcomes . . . As far as I can see, all psychologists, whether they support or oppose some form of reinforcement theory of learning, would agree to this empirical law of effect. (1956, p. 33)

The persistence with which this patched principle has been revered is remarkable. The tenacity with which it has been embraced by its believers is a marvel of an entire generation of psychological history.

The law of effect is demonstrably a circularity. The logical necessity that it contains circular propositions was presented to Psychology by Postman as long ago as 1947. For some reason, this masterful analytical article, with its explicit criticism of the "law" as self-contradictory, had only a faint impression upon the work of more than one psychological theorist. The argument presented by Postman's paper was the obvious argument: that if it is impossible to know whether an event which follows a response is either a "satisfaction" or a "discomfort" until one discovers whether or not the response in question decreases or increases, then one can state no independent definition of those two terms. That is, a word cannot be defined by means of the function or functions ascribed to the event or object which it denotes. A thing is not what a thing does.

It is apparent that the "law" of effect included no logically adequate definitions of its fundamental concepts. As originally proposed, the "law" was nothing other than an exercise in the fraudulent use of language. It is true that certain theorists and critics of theories have sharpened their ability to detect its basic fault; for instance, Osgood wrote:

> It was Thorndike who first clearly incorporated philosophical hedonism within a strictly psychological framework ... Thorndike tried to define [the hypothesis] in terms of observables, and independent of the fact of learning: 'By a satisfying state of affairs is meant one which the animal does nothing to avoid, often doing such things as to attain and preserve it. By a discomforting state of affairs is meant one which the animal avoids and abandons.' It is

usually very difficult to specify when animals
are 'doing things to attain or avoid,' however,
other than observing whether they learn or do
not learn. This underscores the ever-present
danger of tautology in any effect theory. We
cannot explain learning in terms of 'effects' if
these consequences are themselves defined . . .
by the occurrence or non-occurrence of
learning. (1953, pp. 372, 373)

Even in the implied criticism expressed by this and
later appraisals, an attempt has been made to show that
the "law"—although unsound—has contributed to
Psychology much that has been useful in the sense of
pointing the way to facts which must be known about
conditioning. Yet, taken by itself, the "law" of effect
is surely not meaningful and thus cannot be true. A
tautology cannot mean anything.

There is no conceivable way in which one can find out
what something called "reinforcement" exactly is—apart
from what can be found out incidentally from behavioral
change. It has been shown that a dilemma occurs in the
process by which "reinforcement is to be defined. It is at
this point appropriate to alter the operant paradigm to:

Figure 5.

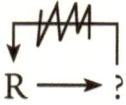

R ⟶ ?

Yet an even more striking dilemma arises when, if one
agrees to a tentative definition of the reinforcement
concept—if one picks out at random some thing or

event to which that name is to be applied—attention is concentrated on the function which such an event is said to have. If a reinforcement can be identified, the problem is: what, in theory, does it do?; of what effects can it be the cause? The object of concern becomes the phenomenon expressed by this symbol

Figure 6.

in the operant equation.

That which follows an event cannot cause the event. This is a formidable fault in the paradigm of operant theory. It has been present in all reinforcement theories of conditioning since the first pronouncement of the "law" of effect gave these theories their origin. Here is a logical error—one which cannot be set aside by scientific data. This is a problem of the *form* taken by a theory.

There is not one reviewer or compiler or part-time critic of conditioning theories in Psychology who has failed to attempt a resolution of the conceptual puzzle of backward action proposed by the "law" which Thorndike so ironically named. Those who have offered constructive interpretations of the paradoxes it presents include Boring, Hilgard, and Osgood; the conclusions of each follow:

> Sometimes it . . . said that this mechanism is 'retroactive,' since the effect, when it is a success, affects the cause; but that is nonsense. Thorndike never meant that the future determined the past, but merely that the traces

of the past were stamped in so that the past might thereafter more readily recur. (Boring, 1957, pp. 562, 563)

[One objection to the "law"] was that the backward effect of a state of affairs on something now past in time is not conceivable . . . The criticism . . . is a faulty one. The effect is revealed in the probability of occurrence of the response when the situation next occurs . . . Translated into more familiar words, Thorndike is saying in this law that rewards or successes further the learning of the rewarded behavior . . . (Hilgard, 1956, p. 20)

There is [a] difficulty which reinforcement theory shares with any 'effect' position . . . How can reinforcement work backward in time? All effect theories state that behaviors are selectively strengthened or weakened on the basis of their consequences . . . Carr (1925) and Hollingworth (1928) have said that the consequence of an act, rather than working backward, works forward to change the stimulus situation on the next trial . . . Although this serves to eliminate the paradox of backward action by making the effect contiguous with the subsequent occurrence of the event, it seems quite incapable of explaining learning under conditions of delayed practice. It is a common procedure, for example, to give subjects a single trial per day. How can the effect of the trial today persist so as to modify the stimulus situation tomorrow? (Osgood, 1953, pp. 380, 381)

The first interpretation, by Boring, was based on a concept of *traces* which is to be taken up later on by this analysis. With respect to Hilgard's position on the subject, the critic's own choice of words permits his interpretation to be dismissed by this: that which "furthers" learning does not cause it. There will be reason to return to the concluding question of Osgood—in the chapter following this one.

A consensus of the several opinions cited recognizes the necessity to alter the reinforcement principle. Each would accomplish this by changing the nature of the argument itself. The puzzle could be made amenable to solution if a reinforcement was no longer considered to have a backward effect. Therefore, it must be considered to have a forward effect.

By means of change in direction of the arrow drawn to show effects of reinforcement in the operant conditioning paradigm, it is possible to derive this incomplete formulation:

Figure 7.

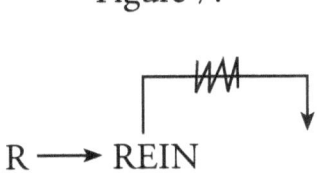

R ⟶ REIN

The structure indicates that a reinforcing stimulus has an effect upon some unstated event which follows that stimulus in time of occurrence. What then comes after a reinforcement that, itself, is produced by a response? In the typical operant experiment, the event in question is a response.

The operant paradigm can now be rewritten by the following equation:

Figure 8.

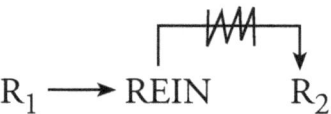

$$R_1 \longrightarrow REIN \qquad R_2$$

The responses have been numbered by subscripts so that they are clearly differentiated. This paradigm indicates that reinforcement produced by one response has an effect upon a subsequent response. The effect is such that it makes R_2 measurably different from R_1; this is just what is meant by behavioral change. Thus—on the surface at least—there is in this paradigm a workable conceptualization of how conditioning of an organism takes place. Its structure implies that, should the second response described be observed to differ from the first in some quantifiable degree such as, for example, reaction time, then an event which can be shown to have intervened between them will be taken to have been the cause of that change. In the fundamental operant demonstration, since a reinforcement is an automatic product of a response, the causal element in the sequence is assumed to be that reinforcement.

On these terms, the operant paradigm is expanded to a point at which it can be said to be logically sound. Two behavioral events are required to fill out the equation. Consider that it is solely the difference between them which is to be explained by this logical reconstruction. The occurrence of neither response has, at this stage of the discussion, been attached to a conceptual element. It is so far only possible to make inferences from the theory about why it is that responses *change* in an orderly manner. Thus not behavior but conditioning has up to now been provided with a meaningful explanation by the reinforcement principle. The omission is clear-cut and will prove decisive.

It is necessary to pause briefly before more intensive analyses of operant theory are begun. To recapitulate what has been said concerning the reinforcement principle, the concept was shown to present two unanswered questions that were implicit in the effect theory it replaced. These were:

1. what is reinforcement?;
2. what is the function of a reinforcement?

The best possible answer to the first question has been to restrict the signification of the term "reinforcement" to a certain homogeneous class of stimulus events; this class would be designated as those stimuli which are known not to be aversive to an organism. Nevertheless, if there is no other criterion for deciding what is and what is not aversive for an organism except what the organism does, there is no sure way for making an identification of this type. Thus one can not know what "reinforcement" means on the basis of these methods of clarification alone. Some concrete defining properties of such an event must be found.

With respect to the second question, the preferred solution has been to propose that, when an event given the name "reinforcement" occurs between two responses, the second response may be found to have differed markedly from the first—for example, its "strength" may have increased. From this point of view, at least a specific *function* has been ascribed to the thing called "reinforcement"; the function ascribed to it is that it causes learning to occur—it conditions. Yet the same causal function could be imputed to something called "X"; there is no reason to denote the causal agent by a specific conceptual term on the evidence as it presently stands. In this sense, an answer to the second question is impossible in the absence of the definition called for by the first. No psychological theory proposed to the time of this writing has given that definition with sufficient clarity.

The preceding discussion has argued that the concept of reinforcement cannot be inferred from behavioral change. That is, it is mistaken to say that, because an organism is learning, it must be receiving "reinforcement" from the environment. These conclusions are purely semantic in nature. It is appropriate to add to the discussion an account of some conceptual maneuvers the theorist might employ to evade difficulties of a system based on the reinforcement principle. One of these would have been applicable had the operant paradigm been left intact—in its original form as:

Figure 9.

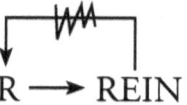

R ⟶ REIN

In order to change the model so that the erroneous backward effect it proposes is eliminated, the following revision can be made:

Figure 10.

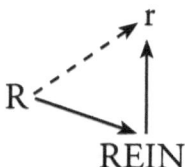

REIN

The equation in this form shows that, although reinforcement is directly produced by a response, the causal action of reinforcement is not on the response itself but on a representation of responding which occurs contemporaneously with an internal counterpart of the overt response that persists until it coincides with a reinforcing event, which then has an effect upon this *internal* representation. Many theorists have referred to such a mechanism and have written postulates to deal with it into their theories. It is the concept of a *response trace*. In the terminology of this book, the paradigm will be described in this way:

Figure 11.

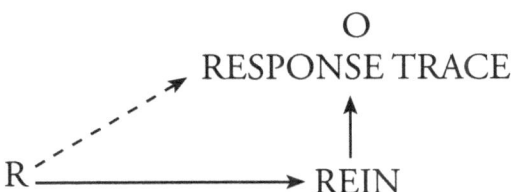

It is apparent that to carry out this revision of the theory, reference must be made to a special class of variables of the organismic category.

Another solution of this type is conceivable when the paradigm is turned around to form

Figure 12.

as worked out in earlier analyses. If a reinforcing stimulus is said to become represented internally, the effect of such a stimulus upon a subsequent response can be explained by *reinforcement stimulus traces* operating within the organism between the two overt events. Thus the paradigm becomes:

Figure 13.

This describes a process by which reinforcement is internalized, persists in time, and exerts a causal influence upon the second of two responses in sequence. This would account for changes in behavior occurring across a temporal interval. The explanation is much the same as those put forward by Carr and Hollingworth, leading to the objection raised by Osgood already reported. In any case, it requires the assumption of a different kind of organismic variable than the one discussed formerly; the revised paradigm should be written:

Figure 14.

This form of the equation indicates that *traces* of the reinforcing event—not of a response—can cause responses to change. The hypothesized organismic variable it incorporates will be found prominent in numerous theories of conditioning.

A third possible strategy would be to combine the two preceding devices into one. This would result in a grand design having this form:

Figure 15.

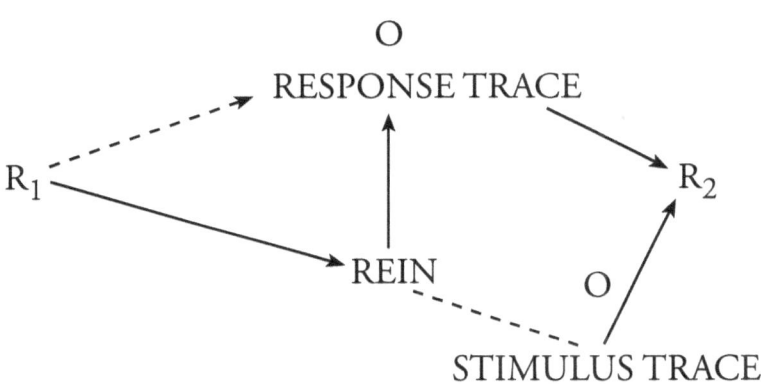

This intricate paradigm resembles, in structure, the omnibus theory of Hull. Its concepts imply that reinforcement has a dual effect upon conditioning: to act upon the trace of a response and to become represented itself in a stimulus trace. It may be that traces of both response and reinforcing stimulus can summate to produce a change in the second response of a sequence. Such an explanation would include hypothetical statements about a probable locus for this summation as well as postulates to account for temporal relationships between the two trace variables. The paradigm described is one that employs the concept of traces to the full extent of its usefulness. The problems it presents are those of any organismic approach to behavior.

None of the attempted solutions just referred to has been chosen by operant theory. There is no provision within the theory for any concept of traces or trace-like representations of overt events. For the operant theorist, a stimulus is a stimulus—an event occurring in the *environment* of an organism; very little attention is paid to the essentially neurological facts of proprioceptive stimulation, and they are referred-to by no postulates of the system. Also for the operant theorist, a response is a response—an event occurring at the *periphery* of an organism, expressed by the movement of a muscle. If such events as these persist in time, that temporal property can be measured independently of measurements made of afferent and efferent circuits, phase sequences in the brain, or digestive processes. The latter are, for the operant conditioner, events of a class which lies outside the boundaries of an objective behavioral science. They are phenomena of the black box.

Because operant theory does not propose trace concepts, it cannot make use of the theoretical devices described to clarify its constructs. The theorist has made a commitment to avoidance of concepts expressing the action of organismic variables. For the operant conditioner, the organism is not a self-moving machine. Therefore these possible answers to questions raised concerning the paradigm are *prevented*:

1. that the effect of reinforcement upon a response is not backward in time but contemporaneous with a response which *persists* in time; that a reinforcing stimulus *persists* in time
2. and carries out a transformation in characteristics of that response which follows it from the characteristics of that response which precedes it;

3. that both interpretations are valid and complementary—implying that the effect of reinforcement is directly felt by the trace of a first response and the differing characteristics of a second response.

There is only one kind of conditioning, according to operant theory. That is reinforced conditioning. The term "reinforcement," Skinner wrote in *Science and Human Behavior*, was borrowed from Pavlov, who had used it to refer to events which strengthen behavior—the word "conditioning" having been coined to refer to such a strengthening. The two theories, classical and operant, diverge on these grounds: for the former, a reinforcing stimulus comes before a response—paired with another, prior stimulus; for the latter, it comes after a response. Continuing, Skinner was led to this conclusion:

> . . . these two cases exhaust the possibilities: an organism is conditioned when a reinforcer (1) accompanies another stimulus or (2) follows upon the organism's own behavior. Any event which does neither has no effect in changing a probability of response. (1953, p. 65)

This is how a theory moves toward the justification of its significance in terms of its own existence. The observer is not led from the maze to light by these sentences by Skinner—taken from the same source:

> A biological explanation of reinforcing power is perhaps as far as we can go in saying why an event is reinforcing. Such an explanation is probably of little help in a functional analysis

> for it does not provide us with any way of
> identifying a reinforcing stimulus as such
> before we have tested its reinforcing power
> upon a given organism. (*Science and Human
> Behavior*, 1953, p. 84)

The choice of a way out of conceptual difficulty is, in this case, an appeal to empirical criteria. That is, if conditioning has occurred in a situation in which a certain stimulus has also been observed to occur, the stimulus in question can qualify as a reinforcer. If it worked then it worked.

It is the argument of the present analysis that the first deficiencies of operant theory are faults in the conceptual structure of the system. They are weaknesses in theory construction. They can only lead to confusion on the part of the student who decides to understand what new truth is being told by the system about conditioning. The weaknesses themselves are, moreover, of a kind that can refute what explanatory novelty the theory has achieved. The following concept demonstrates this:

> If a discriminative stimulus . . . maintains
> responding, the stimulus is a reinforcer . . .
> We shall define a discriminative stimulus as a
> stimulus in the presence of which an operant
> response is reinforced. (Kelleher and Gollub,
> 1962, p. 544)

In the first sentence, it appears that "discriminative stimulus" is being defined as a reinforcing stimulus. Thus the first sentence extends the tautology noted earlier in this discussion. Yet if the second sentence is considered to contain what the writers mean to say, a unique problem is introduced. For then the discriminative stimulus becomes one which precedes behavior. If so, it is an *eliciting* stimulus.

In the expanded, clarified operant paradigm repeated below, it is obvious that the part enclosed by a rectangle is the key concept advanced to explain conditioning:

Figure 16.

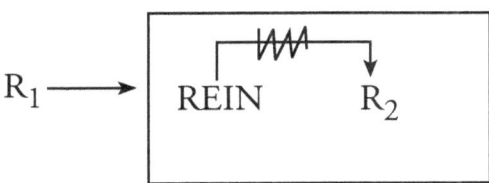

This two-termed description is the explanatory heart of the paradigm, the mechanism that does the work which the theory intends to do. Now if "reinforcement" is translated back into the less sophisticated terminology from which it came, it refers simply to a stimulus. In that sense, the theory returns to the common denominator of Thorndike's connectionism. It becomes, with one difference, a St→R explanation of the most elementary type.

Few operant conditioners would accept the implications of the limiting factors just ascribed to their system. For if reinforcement is no more or less than a unique stimulus, then the operant theorist has contributed less than nothing to psychological knowledge. He has confused the issue severely without being aware of it. Consider that, if the theory tells the student of behavior that certain stimuli can cause a response to differ from a preceding response, it has described the exact means by which classical conditioning takes place. According to that system—as described by Skinner himself—a response is "respondent" and not operant; it is elicited and not emitted; it is elicited or produced or called forth or caused by prior stimulating conditions in the environment of the organism.

For these reasons, the paradigm must always be as if it took the form shown by Figure 17:

Figure 17.

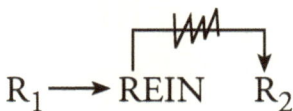

$$R_1 \longrightarrow REIN \quad R_2$$

In this form, it describes not responding but response change; what is to be avoided without exception is this equation: $R_1 \rightarrow REIN \rightarrow R_2$. It has been shown how the ambiguity with which operant concepts are described can be confusing. For by writing as if an operant principle was being referred to, a *respondent* principle is introduced.

These theorists prefer to return to the guiding dogmatisms of their system—with its own peculiar view of causation. They repeat in a hundred varied phrases: behavior is under the control of its consequences. That is impossible.

In the basic operant experiment, the result is a direct function of the way in which the experimental apparatus has been constructed. Yet if such an experimental situation is considered to be a faithful copy of a natural state of affairs, one is led by the paradigm to a very remarkable conclusion about the relationship of an organism to its environment, which is that events in the environment are created by what an organism does.

One does not say—except in a very unfunny metaphor—that an organism "conditions" the environment. That is not what the subject of conditioning is about. It is about how the organism is conditioned. A psychological theory must begin with an account of how the environment takes control of behavior of the organism.

If it is true that first and second responses must differ for conditioning to have occurred, this problem can be approached by focusing attention on first responses. In describing what causes first responses, as with all responses, a preference is shown by operant theorists to use the phrase "consequences" of behavior. Since consequences can not affect anything that has produced them, another concept will have to be inserted. In this case, the concept must provide, finally, a cause for first responses.

Why has the first response of its kind not been provided with a causal explanation by operant theory? The reason is that its cause is hidden among the procedures by which an operant experiment is conducted. These procedures will be discussed in detail in the chapter to follow. In this context, it is important to see that a beginning event in a sequence of behavior is the baseline from which changes are to be measured, a standard against which later responses are to be described by comparison. The single problem remaining for operant theory is to relocate the concept "consequences" at a point in time *before* this response event occurs. The solution is already among unstated propositions of the operant system.

IV. CONTINGENCY

Behavior is never emitted. As with other natural events, a response has a natural origin. However elusive the causes of every response which occurs may prove to discovery, Psychology will have reason to continue until each has been found. To argue by definition for the existence of a certain class of behaviors that is free of causation is to suggest that a truly scientific psychology is impossible.

It is valid to say that a newborn child "emits a cry"; there are also some responses like acts of the fetal organism— such as kicking—which appear to be emitted. That is, they occur for the sake of occurring. Yet that term is most meaningful when defined in much the same way as the physician's term "idiopathic," as applied to a disorder for which there is no presently known cause. Some term has to be reserved to describe the multitudes of behavioral events which psychological theory cannot now explain. "Emitted" is as good as any in defense of ignorance.

There are difficulties in assigning exact denotative meanings to the concepts of elicitation and emission. In spite of this limiting consideration, it is possible to work with definitions such as these: "response" means the movement of a muscle or major muscle-group; "emitted response" means unexplained muscular movements; "elicited response" means explained muscular movements. These decisions do not imply that the first response of a given kind can be called "emitted" at the start and is to be called "elicited" later on when a theory gets around to explaining it. A comprehensive theory of behavior must explain a first response immediately upon its occurrence. Thus it must describe the response as if it had been elicited.

A number of deficiencies of formal structure, scope or comprehensiveness, and just plain sense have been noted with regard to reinforcement theories in general. The most pronounced of these reach their culminations in the Skinnerian system. If one were to look for a primary fault upon which the rest depend, the crucial error was the determination to proceed as if an organism can emit behavior.

Once a first response had been dismissed from their attention, operant conditioners had no choice but to give their attention to the subject of behavioral *change*. To make this distinction relevant to the problem of the emitted response, it is necessary to see that the operant conception of learning is process-oriented. The problem for an operant conditioner working with a rat in a Skinner box is to get behavior "going" in some way. Once this is done, an operant experiment can begin. In it, acquisition proceeds by the gradual addition of more and more nearly "correct" movements and the elimination of movements irrelevant to the specific pattern required. This is what is meant by "shaping" behavior; it is in every sense a process—one by which response events advance steadily toward a criterion. As the observer of these events, the operant conditioner can only concentrate upon the *process;* that is, how each element varies from the one before. His view of the changes which take place in the situation is molar. He sees a total configuration of change.

Consider the concept "contingency"; for a definition of this term, there is no better source than a glossary appended to *Schedules of Reinforcement* that contains the official vocabulary of the operant system:

> 'contingency' . . . In operant conditioning: the temporal, intensive, and topographical conditions under which a response is followed by a positive or negative reinforcing stimulus or the removal of either of these. (1957, p. 725)

The definition is less than resoundingly clear. The key word "conditions" enough resembles "conditioning" to suggest that something is being referred to which has to do with the causes of learning. Whatever the nature of a contingency, it is apparent at this point that it is an event occurring *before* both response and reinforcing stimulus.

The concept of contingency as a principle within operant theory is one of the least elaborated of its constructs. The word is mentioned only occasionally in *Behavior of Organisms,* and the reader of *The Analysis of Behavior* is not manipulated in such a way that it becomes part of his verbal repertoire. The concept has no direct counterpart in any other theory. Thus the task at hand is as one would proceed in the presence of a mystery one is confident that sense will solve.

This examination of the characteristics of a contingency is not made easier by various descriptions which are scattered here and there in operant theoretical writing. One of these is the following: "So far as the organism is concerned, the only important property of the contingency is temporal. The reinforcer simply *follows* the response,"; the statement is from *Science and Human Behavior* (1953, p. 85). In this, it is obvious that a contingency is equated with the occurrence of reinforcement. That means it cannot occur until behavior has taken place; if so, it can have no effect upon the behavior in question.

A contingency must be other than an event that is response-produced or an event the occurrence of which is response-inferred. The concept is most meaningful when interpreted on a par with the concept *possibility*. If one goes into a library to look among the books there, a possibility exists that a book will be found that he will decide to read and will later enjoy. The possibility of pleasure from reading this book exists before the library is entered. To this possibility various criteria of proof or disproof may be applied; yet the most conclusive verification will not be applicable until one has entered the library, etc.. This suspension is a predecessor of every act—in fact, of all natural events, because nothing is not possible.

If every response presupposes the possibilities of its own effect upon the environment, it may be that certain of these possibilities are more likely than others to lead to a given response. This is what the concept of contingency implies in the context of an operant explanation. For the theory, it is the *possibility* of a reinforcement which governs the choice of a particular response from the repertoire. The decisive identifying mark of a contingency is that it comes *before* behavior. Behavior that is contingent has not yet happened; only the contingency of its happening exists.

More than one critic of operant conditioning has taken apart this logical discrepancy, confounded by vague theoretical writing. Thus the term "contingency" was translated by Grünbaum to "expectation" (1953, p. 770) and by Scriven to "disposition" (1956, pp. 121, 122). The preference here is for a term which implies less than these that the responding organism is an active participant in the event. In the case of either expecting or having a disposition, the organism is the expecter or the one disposed. Even the operant theorist would argue that a contingency *originates* in and is a part of the environment of an organism.

The problem of contingency is another among those puzzles of structure that have confronted this analysis so many times before. Given an element of the theory, it is necessary to see how it fits in the framework of that theory; or, where it must be put to give the model an intelligibility it has lacked. It is appropriate to insert the concept of contingency into its correct position in the operant paradigm. Note that there is only one place where it can go—before a response whose contingency it is.

To review, an analogy was drawn between referents of the two terms "contingency" and "possibility"; the purpose of this was not to make the concept of a contingency vulnerable to criticism, but to show that the concept is only sensible in operant theory in some such form as the one presented. In effect, "contingency" was redefined: the circumstance that a state of affairs is possible. This circumstance is, for the organism, an intangible but inescapable condition of uncertainty, a state of not knowing. For its object, a contingency is simply the unknown thing beforehand.

This is the logical status of a contingency. A contingency is a possible state of affairs that behavior can confirm or disprove. This derivation allows for translation of the dictum of Keller and Schoenfeld, which states that learning is the result of "the influence of the outcome of a response upon its strength," to read as follows: learning results from the prior possibility of the outcome of a response. Further, the principle "behavior is under the control of its consequences" becomes: behavior is under the control of the potentiality of its consequences—its contingency.

In considering a contingency as a state of not-knowing, the inference is not to be drawn that the possibilities present in a situation are unknowable. To return to the example of the prospective browser, the person who prepared the library may have provided every conceivable book that he might enjoy. This person would be in a position to know with certainty the inevitable result of his going there to find a book. By contrast, the *user* of the library can know no more than the potential consequences of doing this or that, if he is to be said to be acting as the result of contingency when he enters. The person who has arranged a contingency for another is omniscient. By contrast, the one who is under the control of contingency lacks information.

It will be important to keep a careful accounting—in the analyses to follow—of the characters used to exemplify operant principles. The part each is said to play must be examined to reveal its contribution to the explanatory pattern. The *procedure* of an operant conditioning experiment will be investigated thoroughly. The object is to see what goes on in an operant laboratory. The goal will be a description of its methods of data collection.

Experimental psychologists were once profoundly affected by certain developments in the natural sciences that came to be known as operationism. The name suggests a theory or approach or movement, yet while the concepts of operationism became the subject of a vigorous debate, they did not become the basis of a theory of science. Derived from logical positivism out of relativity/uncertainty theory, Bridgman's proposals fell short of changing scientific method. As Stevens (1939) and others have noted, there was very little in operationism that would reveal to a scientist how to proceed to discover meaningful data; rather, the arguments of operationism referred to the *definitional* statements made by scientists about the variables under investigation by research. The use of terminology which could be called operational is a technique in the construction of theory from data, or in the practical journalistic problem of writing about what has happened in an experiment.

The fascination that operationism held for most early behaviorists was the curious result of an interpretation Bridgman did not intend. The false impression somehow was conveyed that this physicist had advocated stringent new rules for the way in which an experiment should be conducted—that the activities of the experimenter himself should become more rigidly self-conscious and objectively measurable. It seemed to many that operationism focused new attention on *what people do* in a laboratory as opposed to, for instance, an ion or a bacillus in the same laboratory; the interpretation persisted in psychological writing, as in this example by Deese: "An operational definition of a term, in the simplest use, is a description of the operations performed by an experimenter or observer . . ." (1958, p. 5).

It is fortunate for Psychology that this interpretation of operationism did not lead to experiments on the conducting of experiments. In time, it was apparent that the operationists had not argued that a scientific variable equals what a scientist does in relation to it; rather, the argument implied that the definition of a scientific term is the *measurement* made of its referent. Thus it could be seen that Bridgman had not opened the way for a new order on the part of scientists, nor had changed by a fraction what is done by a scientist in a laboratory. By its most just evaluation, Bridgman's contribution was to intensify the *precision* of the descriptive—that is, verbal—behavior of scientists about their subjects of study.

Operant theorists have spent much effort in the attempt to express, in objectively measurable terms, each of the constructs of their system. This outspoken drive for precision in terminology led some to give the name "operational behaviorism" to the theory. To a certain extent, the rigorous standards of definition set by this school have left their mark on modern Psychology. It has been shown how poorly defended the theory becomes when this rigor breaks down—as in the case of the concept of reinforcement, although the problems of that concept were present in the theories from which it had been borrowed. The difficulties into which the operant system has fallen are not primarily those of data description. Its major deficiencies were occasions of carelessness in theory construction.

The analysis to follow will work first with a step-by-step account of the typical operant demonstration—presented in more complete form than previously so that no single event will be missed. The problem is not to see what happens from the vantage of a psychologist who observes behavior in a laboratory; rather as one who, having examined a paradigm based on the demonstration, knows that something must happen there for which the theory has no provision. One knows that:

1. a rat is put in a box;
2. the rat may not have been put in such a box before in its life;
3. a mechanism outside the box has been set to drop a pellet of food into the box under certain conditions;
4. a pellet of food will be dropped into the box only if a lever projecting into the box from one wall is depressed at a slight angle;
5. the rat may hesitate for a time before coming in contact with the bar and depressing the bar; e.g., it may hesitate for seven minutes and nine seconds;
6. when the bar is depressed, out drops a pellet of food; the rat may eat the food.

When this has occurred, imagine that the rat is taken from the experimental box and allowed for a short while to explore the laboratory table. Part one comes to an end.

In due course, the rat is retrieved from table and returned to box. After a period of hesitation, e.g., lasting one minute and three seconds, rat depresses bar a second time. Again a pellet of food drops and is eaten. Again, removal of rat from box is performed. From this description, the following list of events can be compiled: two responses; two response latencies—differing in duration by 366 seconds; two "reinforcement" events; two eating or "consummatory" responses, one interval between occasions of rat in box. It is possible here to refer to the operant paradigm to see how the model would integrate—if it cannot yet explain—the occurrences described; this is the form that the equation takes:

Figure 18.

The consummatory responses included in the list are left out because they make the paradigm more complex than it need be; the second reinforcement in the sequence is left out for the same reason. The question marks refer to still-unknown events which directly cause the responses. The upper arrow leading from reinforcement to the second response indicates that, as a function of a prior reinforcing stimulus, response two will be found to differ from response one. In the situation as described, this explanation is directly meaningful: its point of reference is to the 366 seconds by which latency of bar-pressing behavior has shortened. It can then be said that the reinforcement in question has had an effect upon behavioral change to a degree expressed by that temporal phenomenon.

Now focus closer attention on one other of the events described; the interval between trials or the two appearances of rat in box. That is, one of the question marks in the paradigm can be at least provisionally replaced by an identifying mark. This is the second question mark, the one after reinforcement and before response two.

The paradigm then reads:

Figure 19.

$$? \longrightarrow R_1 \longrightarrow REIN \begin{bmatrix} \quad\quad\quad\quad \end{bmatrix} R_2$$

The analysis will concentrate on the empty place indicated by brackets with no concept to fill them. Whatever is required to bridge the opening will refer to some event or events occurring during a transitional period between two stages of conditioning. To bring this interval into sharp focus, imagine that the rat is not allowed to roam on an experimental table between trials; instead, it is taken from the box and returned at once to its home cage; the rat is left there overnight—twelve hours—before being returned to box next day. None of the other events described has to be omitted or revised. The paradigm, then, contains an unfilled space referring to the fact that rat is absent from box for a twelve-hour interval. Note that also, in the paradigm presented, there is no arrow leading from reinforcement to the second response. The central problem has become: how can the interval be filled with some event that will ensure that reinforcement does, in reality, cause responses to change?

During the long wait at home, a rat may recall the curious circumstances of the day before and all that they might mean. What had begun as a trip outside the cage had proved a short-lived freedom, for it had found itself transported swiftly to another cell. Yet this one had no bars, a roof that one could look through, and the shiniest of new walls. There had been only two odd arrangements in the design of this new "cage": a leg or tail protruding through a hole and another opening that might or might not have been a tunnel leading outside. In the course of a cautious tour of his strange space, a singular incident occurred. When investigating the area around the leg, a careless step had led to a sudden slip and fall, broken only by the leg itself. This object proved no leg at all; it was made of metal and promptly gave way. The rat had come down with a thump against the hard grid flooring. On opening its eyes and recovering its bearings, it had smelled a familiar aroma. There in the tunnel opening— surprise of surprises—was food, and it had soon been eaten. Before being allowed a moment's speculation on the meaning of this decidedly unusual progression of events, there had been that brusque dismissal from the new home and banishment to the old one again. Very odd, very odd indeed. With a few hastily-drawn inferences, it may conclude: metal object has something to do with food; but, for some reason, the object must be moved before any result is achieved.

A rat does not think, reflect, reason or plan—according to operant theory. If there is no provision in the operant vocabulary for saying that an organism "remembers what happened the last time," the paradigm cannot imply that other significant events beside reinforcement occur between responses. That is, the interval can not be filled in with the concept:

Figure 20.

O

THOUGHT

This would require reference to one form of organismic variable—no form of which is acceptable. By arguing in this way, the theorist remains faithful to the traditions of behaviorism. This restriction does not apply only to rats; it applies to all organisms. If it did not, the theory could be worth nothing.

A thoroughgoing behavioristic conception of the organism denies "consciousness" to rat and human. Thus operant theory does not propose to explain how aware an organism is about what it is doing when it is doing something. In the operant demonstration, the rat is not "conscious" of pressing a bar—either by accident or intentionally. Thus, after the interval in question, it can not enter the experimental situation with "set" or scheme; it has not "figured out" anything. This means the rat does not carry, within itself, a representation of the fact that before, in similar circumstances, food had appeared. In other words, no "presence" of prior reinforcement is maintained when rat is returned to box—at least, it is not present in a cognitive sense. Images are missing from the situation. Whatever a reinforcement may be said to contribute to the organism's attempting to learn, it takes other forms than the dream of food.

When the interval between experimental sessions ends and rat has just *returned* to box, there is a moment of uncertainty that becomes crucial for the observer. One who watches the first few seconds might well ask:

1. will it press the bar?;
2. will it press the bar after less time than before?

These are questions which serve to summarize the many problems of the operant demonstration. The explanatory system of operant conditioning fails to make plain the requisite information in this case. Of course, one can generalize to any specific case from what has happened in the case of another rat in a comparable situation. Yet that is not the test of a paradigm. This analysis has found no basis in operant theory for the observer to say with certainty—at the critical point—what an individual rat is going to do. Should the observer take for granted that the rat will do A, there is no basis on which he can with certainty say when.

Still more information is sought. The search must proceed with one more thorough probe into the procedures of an operant experiment. One of the routines of the laboratory will be worth noting. In the between-session interval, when the rat is safely locked away at home, a vital event occurs; no food is given the rat, a commonplace incident yet one full of meaning to the problem under discussion. The interval is filled with deprivation.

Deprivation is an *operation* performed by an experimenter upon an experimental animal. It consists in withholding food, water, etc., from the animal or in removing such objects from an animal once permitted free access to them. It must be emphasized that to deprive an organism of something constitutes a procedure or operation. The problem remaining is to show that this event is *causal*.

If, in the demonstration described, a rat is put back in its home cage for twelve hours between trials, certain temporary arrangements will have been made for its stay there. A food-tray will have been removed and this tray will not be filled with food and replaced at any time during the twelve hours. Consider the case in which this precaution is *not* taken. The rat might be confronted, during the interval, with a limitless supply of food from which it could sample as it liked throughout the night. Taking advantage of the opportunity, the rat might stuff itself until satiated when morning came. The result of this will be obvious to anyone who has watched animal behavior only casually. Whether allowed to remain in its cage or dumped into an experimental apparatus, the well-fed rat sleeps.

A satiated animal will not perform as expected in any conditioning situation. This means that in order to induce it to learn, the animal must to some extent have been starved, parched, prevented from having sexual stimulation, etc.; then it is ready to be put into an apparatus in which learning is possible. That depends upon previous events which consist in removing from an organism something that organism needs. To do this is to deprive.

The preparation of animals for learning is a human task nearly as old as experimental psychology. Before conditioning was even the ostensible subject of an experiment and when the apparatus was a puzzle-box, the first behaviorist invented a method for bringing animals under control. Thorndike wrote:

> So far as possible the animals were kept in a uniform state of hunger which was practically utter hunger; that is, no cat or dog was experimented on, when the experiment involved any important question of fact or theory, unless I was sure that his motive was of the standard strength, (*vid.*: Dennis, 1948, pp. 380, 381)

In this description, the word "motive" is out of place; it will be discussed later on in the chapter. It is clear that the discovery of the "law" of effect took place in a laboratory environment in which deprivation played an important part. For the most recent of the many descendants of this approach, the art has become considerably refined—even to the point at which deprivation can be directly *measured* and, thus, becomes one of the data of an experiment. A comment by Scriven describes what happens in operant conditioning:

> Skinner starves his pigeons to 80 percent of their *ad lib* weight; he is fortunate that such a simple procedure yields workable results. We may expect . . . that with higher organisms this regimen will not yield quite such high intra-species predictability. (1956, p. 103)

Although Scriven's conclusion is the right one, here it can only serve as a preface to a discussion of the generality of the effects of deprivation on conditioning. The next object will be to find out in what way reinforcement and deprivation are related.

Deprivation fits the conceptual structure in the following way:

Figure 21.

In this equation, deprivation is shown simply as an event that intervenes between a reinforcement and a second response. Because depriving of food is the opposite of giving food, a rat satiated with food will not press a bar to get food—in fact, will do very little. Deprivation must be related to the occurrence of the second response.

The paradigm becomes:

Figure 22.

The second response in a sequence is now attached to its immediate cause. It is now possible to see why an animal responds in an operant demonstration if the sequence of trials is broken by a temporal interval. If deprivation is carried out, then the second response of a particular class will follow.

The observer's other request for information depends upon a positive answer, to a more basic question. The occurrence of first responses of a class is not explained by any reinforcement theory. This is an artifact of the structure of these theories, one which derives from the misplaced position of reinforcing events in relation to behavior. For the one thing an organism has not experienced *before* R_1 is performed is reinforcement. To say that behavior occurs for the *purpose of* being reinforced was the original error. To propose that behavior occurs because it occurs is to take error to its extreme.

Before the operant demonstration begins, the rat to be studied in a Skinner box is deprived. Deprivation—if food is taken away—is continued until the rat's weight has been reduced to some fraction of its normal weight. Only when this criterion of malnutrition has been reached is the animal ready to learn to press a bar. This means that deprivation is a preliminary requisite for operant conditioning. If it should not be administered, an operant experiment would begin and end with a demonstration of somnolence in *rattus rattus*. Many years ago Skinner wrote:

> [One] factor producing a change in strength is, of course, sleep. It is observed when records are taken for several hours and appears as an abrupt change in the rate of responding from any value then in force to a value of zero. Whether or not the rat falls asleep at such a time has not been determined by direct observation, (1938, p. 417)

It follows that if satiation is an agent of sleep, activity is a function of deprivation.

The repaired operant paradigm can now be written as follows:

Figure 23.

$$D_1 \longrightarrow R_1 \longrightarrow REIN \left[\quad D_2 \longrightarrow R_2 \right.$$

The term "reinforcement" can be given an independent definition: an event which follows upon deprivation in the operant conditioning situation. The deprivation procedure and the concept of contingency are one. If "contingency" is defined as an event or set of events that precede or precedes behavior, this term refers to the deprivation of an organism that occurs before it is placed in a situation in which a response can be performed. A prior arrangement made with respect to an animal's behavior is finalized when the response in question leads to a reinforcing event.

Deprivation is a kind of plan for getting animals to move about. Raising the general level of activity will, in the operant situation, lead to bar-pressing. This is all that is required, at present, as explanation of why an organism does what it does. Now in the case of behavior change or learning, it is necessary to show why responses *differ* throughout a series—why presses of a bar become more efficient, forceful, and above all more rapid in a Skinner box.

This analysis will present a final version of the operant paradigm, stretched to a limit beyond which it could not be recognized as such. The following paradigm emerges:

Figure 24.

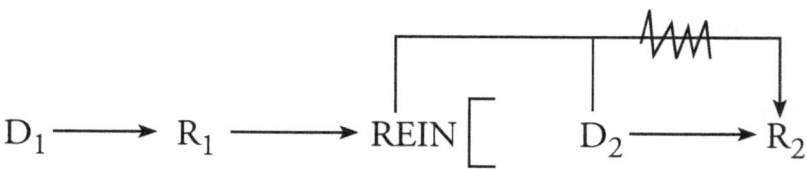

$$D_1 \longrightarrow R_1 \longrightarrow REIN \left[\quad D_2 \longrightarrow R_2 \right.$$

The full equation attempts to explain both responding and response change. In such a paradigm;

1. D_2 must have a more direct effect upon R_2 than REIN;
2. the effects of D_2 and REIN upon R_2 cannot be additive.

The relationship between reinforcement and deprivation is *subtractive*. The two events do not complement each-other but cancel each-other out. What deprivation accomplishes in preparing an animal for learning, reinforcement works to remove. Thus what causes learning is deprivation minus reinforcement. A concise definition of "reinforcement" is an event that reduces deprivation.

The reinforcement just defined is of the "positive" kind. Thus "non-reinforcement" denotes an event that maintains deprivation. Further, it is obvious that, in the operant demonstration, positive reinforcement is given to an animal in very small quantities. Massive deprivation of food is only minimally relieved by each pellet obtained from pressing a bar. Thus, in the basic experimental situation, conditions of non-reinforcement are prevalent over positive reinforcing conditions. Here at last is a clue to what factors are operating when the experiment is elaborated to investigate other contingencies than the simplest one. When schedules of reinforcement are established before responses occur in a Skinner box, conditions of non-reinforcement "control" behavior better than continuous reinforcement because they restore deprivation time and again.

No one has summarized the relevant data more succinctly than Deese did in these words:

> . . . the rate at which rats in a Skinner box press the lever depends upon their state of hunger at the moment . . . The more food the rat eats before the experiment, the lower its rate of response. This general effect is also true whether or not the rat is reinforced. (1958, pp. 100, 101)

It turns out that the operant approach is the most fully elaborated system of deprivation conditioning that experimental psychology has produced.

Deprivation conditioning has not been identified as such by those few theorists who have conducted a full-scale examination of Skinnerian writing. Although Deese indicated that he was at least half-aware of what factors are at work in an operant experiment, he was led to a conclusion which can only be described as half-hearted. His lame summary statement on the subject was the following: " . . . we find B.F. Skinner generally classified as a learning theorist, though he is very little concerned with learning and memory. With considerably more justification he could be called an incentive theorist." (1958, p. 322)

Many psychological theories have used reinforcement variables to explain conditioning and, at the same time, have included among their concepts ones which take account of the facts of deprivation. These theories sharing common elements have often been classified as the "need reduction" or "drive reduction" group. Among them, Hull's omnibus system was the most elaborate. While there can be such need-state theories in Psychology for as long as the science continues, it is to the credit of operant theorists that they have shown the way to a permanent cure for the malady.

For the operant conditioner, only one kind of data is acceptable to Psychology: events occurring at the *periphery* of the organism. This is clear in a statement found in the earliest of Skinner's theorizing, namely:

> The 'drive' is a hypothetical state interpolated between operation and behavior and is not actually required in a descriptive system. (1938, p. 368)

This is the kind of remark that led Boring to take note of a popular expression denouncing the peripheralistic approach as a "Psychology of the empty organism"

(1950, p. 650). Yet when the operation referred to is no other than deprivation, the organism, when prepared for an operant experiment, in a much less rhetorical sense is an empty one.

The operant conditioner gets rats to respond by starving them. Thus, he knows very well if they will do *something*. There is no necessity for the conditioner himself to take detailed readings of stomach contractions or neural correlates of these. Nevertheless, since operant theory does not admit to controlling by depriving, it must transfer internal states to some other non-physiological locus. This is done by making motivation a response-inferred concept. The following frame from a *programmed textbook* is an example of how this is done; "correct" answers are in italics:

> Popular explanations of behavior frequently employ words like 'want,' 'desire,' or 'need.' The observable referent for these words is usually a high *rate* of responding. In such cases they *are not* really causes of the response rate. (Holland and Skinner, 1961, p. 193)

In this formulation, one can know if a particular "state" of the organism has been established only after the fact—one must wait until it does one thing or another.

On these terms, a man was hungry because he has eaten. This example is paraphrased from Skinner's own rejection (1953, p. 31) of the need/state hypothesis by operant theory. There could be no clearer reason for designating the operant approach as a "radical behaviorism." To transform hunger from a physiological state into a record of ingestive responses is to take the most extreme stand against all physicalistic descriptions.

To recapitulate the preceding pages in which the deprivation principle has been examined, these facts were presented:

1. no counterpart of the *treatment* of the animal as it appears in other theories is to be found within the operant model of conditioning; in some form or other, the missing concept must be supplied;

2. the omission results in part from the theory's commitment to considering behavior as "emitted" or uncaused; if a response has *no* cause, then there is no reason to assume that deprivation could be related to a response in a causal manner;

3. no organismic variables of the central physiological or neurological type are given a place in the operant system; therefore, events of those classes are not measured directly in operant experiments, and there are consequently no conceptual elements representing them in the paradigm.

The discussion concluded by showing that problems posed by the clash of fact with ideology have left operant theorists with no recourse but to take the severest possible position on the subject of deprivation. The theory has argued that "states" such as hunger—even in infrahuman animals—may not exist at all. For, the theory argues, they can like "consciousness" be identified by inductive inference from overt behavioral events.

As far as hunger is concerned, it cannot be assigned the same scientific status as is given the atom. It is a familiar condition, along with certain other appetites, and its efficient causes are well known. It is one thing to describe "thoughts" only by inference from overt responses; it is a very different thing to say that a stimulus which follows a response is "reinforcing" depending upon what happens subsequently to the strength of that response; the theoretical dilemma that the latter reasoning presents has been thoroughly analyzed in this book. Yet, to resort to a response-inferred derivation of deprivation is out of the question entirely. In a report of an operant experiment, the methods by which an animal has been deprived beforehand are fully catalogued. Trouble arises when these procedures are classified simply as "operations" and left at that—as if that designation somehow excluded these events from being included in any explanation of what the experiment reveals.

The practice of attempting to frame scientific explanations based upon second-order inferences is as pointless and sad as the tears of a Bedouin whose camel has died. There is no excuse for this kind of makeshift theorizing in any rigorously objective science. Often, those who argue most stridently that a fact must be taken as a concrete fact, are those who retreat to higher levels of abstraction when inconsistencies are shown in the theoretical structures they have proposed. The operant conditioner is not being accused here of disingenuousness but of an acute narrowing of vision no serious scientist can afford. The same kind of evaluation of the sources of error in the theory is evident in Scriven's analysis of the concept of satiation—as follows:

> . . . it is this basic process in science—the process of ascribing states to substances and organisms—which forms the first level of theory-building; and it is one that Skinner cannot avoid himself, for example, when he

describes an organism as 'satiated.' This term would have to be abandoned even if Skinner's data was [*sic*] still accepted, if we did not believe that the gratification had produced an effect on the organism that, in fact, persisted. Our reason for thinking this is true is the change in response frequency after unrestricted eating . . . is allowed, when the reinforcement is food. This striking result . . . shows clearly that an effect has persisted on the organism. Let us call this effect 'satiation'; it is a state of the organism. Now, Skinner overlooks the theoretical element in this analysis and imagines he can define the word without any reference to state: he views it as a summary of past history . . . one cannot believe the past history to affect the present behavior except via a present state—and science *as a whole* . . . must explain how this implicit hypothesis . . . is justified. (1956, p. 124)

After working his painstaking way through the labyrinth, Scriven arrives once more at his own remedy for the problem of deprivation/satiation—the concept of "dispositions." He concludes, from his analysis, that the dilemmas of operant theory, as conceptualized, are insurmountable. Without intending irony, his conclusion is offered to the psychologist as a full justification for "neurologically-oriented" research. This is not necessarily the only way out of the box. Psychology can be a science of behavior in fact as well as in name.

At this point it is important to review what is left of the operant contribution in order to see, in perspective, its significance for modern Psychology. This kind of appraisal has a counterpart in the contribution of Freud. Just as Freud's work has given totally *practical methods* for changing the behavior of people who are ill, there was erected around these methods a theory of mental process that has failed to withstand tests of analysis. By contrast, operant ideology has little of practical value to recommend to anyone who is not a professional circus trainer. What lesson is there in the operant way of looking at psychological problems?

The operant credo teaches the psychologist to pay attention to responses—what an organism does. This kind of singleness of view is claimed to cut through and eliminate many traditional deterministic conceptions. Consider that the human individual was once said to be a product of fate and other supernatural forces. More recently the individual has been said to be a product of socio-economic determinants, of region and of class. Throughout history, the individual has been said to be a product of hereditary background. Operant behaviorism set aside these pessimisms with the dogma that the individual is a self-activating mechanism. The first accomplishment of operant theory was to free the organism from deterministic bonds. For the operant conditioner, an organism does what it does: significant behavior of which it is capable simply emerges, appears. It is instructive to observe how this doctrine has evolved through the course of the past seventy-six years. In the concluding chapter of *Behavior of Organisms*, it appeared in this form:

> Operant behavior clearly satisfies a definition
> based upon what the organism is doing to the
> environment, and the question arises whether

it is not properly the main concern of a student
of behavior . . . (1938, p. 438)

At that stage in the development of the hypothesis,
the organism was seen as not only responding on its
own—"emitting" behavior—but as actively producing
changes in the surround.

There is no question but that operant doctrine has
progressed at an ever-increasing rate away from its unique
position on determinism. The theory is no longer based
on what the organism is "doing to the environment";
it asserts exactly the opposite. For operant theory, the
organism is *a product* of control.

As written, operant theory lacks a motivational
postulate. The organism is, for it, controlled by
the possible acquisition of an entirely hypothetical
reinforcing event. This means that the organism is seen
as "pulled" and not "pushed," as is the case with a donkey
who follows a carrot tied to its harness. The description
implies that behavior is performed *to get* this or that
object. The fallacy here will not be obscure to one who
is equipped with carrot and well-fed donkey. An apple
may fall to the ground because of its weight, because it
is dislodged from a tree, and because of gravity. These
circumstances are present before the fall. An apple does
not fall in order *to get* nearer the center of the Earth.

If a magnet attracts iron filings, it does so because
a causal chain of events is set off that culminates in
movements of molecules of the filings in the direction
of the magnet. One says these objects are being "pulled"
because they go toward another object which is said to
be pulling them. Yet this terminology has to do with
position and movement—the phenomenon is one of
going forward. When something "pulls" another thing

to itself, it is only that the distance between them decreases. This could be considered an instance in which "pull" is used in a topographical or spatial sense. When cause-and-effect relationships are referred to, the terms "pull" and "push" must be redefined if they are to be applied. A cause can be said to "push" its effect. That is, an effect does not call upon or "pull" its causal event. The transaction is carried out in one "direction" only—for the "direction" in question is temporal as well as spatial and only time cannot go backward. Thus an analogy has been drawn between the notion of behavior done *to get* something and an invalid conception of "pull" in cause-effect relations.

Without a motivational postulate, a psychological theory will find survival hard. In fact, a scientific explanation requires concepts of how its machinery is driven, a power of which it originates. When a science is charged with telling why a certain natural event occurs, it cannot begin with description and end with correlation. It must proceed to the discovery of dynamic relationships—until it stops just short of vitalisms. It has been shown in earlier chapters of this book that the concept of the motive has, traditionally in Psychology, been stated in terms of organismic variables of one kind or another. With few exceptions, motives have been considered as residing *inside* an organism—as something possessed by the organism. This kind of theory is to the operant conditioner hopelessly old-fashioned; he has done his best to leave it far behind. The problem unsolved is this; how to get the motive outside.

A motive as an event occurring in the environment of the organism is a concept that plays tricks with the imagination. One is accustomed to talking about—with respect to causes of human behavior—the motive as an *inward* spur to action, a kind of physical or mental turmoil which, on some signal, causes action. There is nevertheless some history of explaining motivated behavior in terms of external "triggers" of action. For the sociologist, a person is exposed to pressure from cultural and group influences; he is made to do what he does to satisfy demands of a *milieu* in which he finds himself; his behavior is said to be motivated by a society. Ethologists of the "imprinting" school hold that, in certain infrahuman species, particular stimuli occurring at critical periods in the life cycle act as "releaser" mechanisms for behavior; these are specific and immediate causal events that can be considered external sources of motivation to the organism. The psychologists Dollard and Miller theorized that strong stimuli in the environment constitute motivational events for the organism; this hypothesis had some success in explaining why certain human as well as infrahuman behavior occurs.

These formulations more or less satisfy specifications for a non-physicalistic, *external* concept of motive—whether what is motivating for each is *milieu*, special stimuli, or especially intense stimuli. The important contribution, taken collectively, is that they see the organism as *being* motivated and not *containing* motives. They propose causal elements that are prior to behavior and thus *can* be causal. These elements function to push—since they cannot pull—the organism this way and that. Although operant behavior ostensibly is done *to get*, for example, food, it is in reality done *because of an absence of food*. Thus depriving an organism motivates it. As it happens, depriving an animal is one of the least-well understood of scientific operations. A laboratory technician reaches up to a rat's cage and removes a tray of food. That is just about all that has been discovered concerning the phenomenon.

Depriving an animal is *not*:

1. reinforcing the animal—in fact the opposite of that;
2. a stimulus—although it may produce, apart from weight loss, stimuli the animal can sense;
3. a motive—in the sense of something the animal has with it or about it; rather, it is an event which motivates.

Deprivation is a response. Behavior of the operant rat is controlled by behavior of the operant technical assistant. If this person fails to deprive, an experimental organism refuses to perform. If behaviorism had paid attention to human beings, this obvious truth might have been more plain. An explanation of behavior in the operant demonstration will be based on a paradigm which shows that the behavior of one organism is followed by the behavior of another—a relationship is completed.

V. OPERANT CONDITIONING

Learning is the effect of forces that originate in an environment. It is meaningful to say that a contingency causes behavioral change if understood as the removal of some object an organism requires. A question has been raised about whether or not such a principle can be said to apply to organisms occupying all levels of the phylogenetic scale. An answer to that question will be presented in the chapters to follow.

The paradigm that explains conditioning in an operant demonstration is most precisely designated as follows:

Figure 25.

$$R \longrightarrow R_1 \longrightarrow R \qquad\qquad R \longrightarrow R_2 \longrightarrow R$$
$$\text{DEPRIVING}_1 \quad \text{REINFORCING}_1 \mid\mid \text{DEPRIVING}_2 \quad \text{REINFORCING}_2$$

The paradigm can be made more intelligible if restricted to the *occurrence* of behavior instead of behavioral change. In effect, the paradigm can be stated without reference to the learning phenomenon. The following form is derived:

Figure 26.

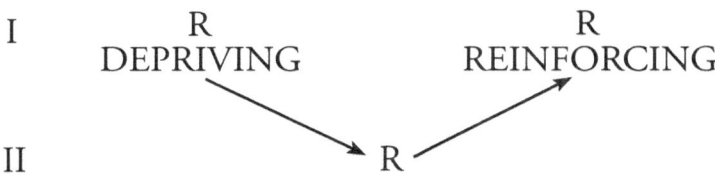

This paradigm indicates that a response of one organism (*II*) follows deprivation behavior and precedes the reinforcement behavior of another organism (*I*). The paradigm does not intend to imply that behavioral relationships occur on multiple "levels"; it is designed to show related responses occurring at two loci or from two directions.

The present discussion principally concerns the relationship between behavior *per se* and its cause, as illustrated here:

Figure 27.

To see this description take place in action, it is necessary to observe two organisms, each capable of receiving some information generated by the other's responses. Observe that the first organism (*I*) behaves in a manner having to do with taking away something from the other's environment or in barring the other from something in the environment. Since, according to reinforcement theory, what is being manipulated is positive reinforcement or its absence, it can be said that the depriving by *I* has the nature of a *promise* of reinforcement (see also Kohn (1993, pp. 12-14).

The depriving procedure is one by which *I* promises something to *II*. It is important that:

1. the promise entails that *II* perform a certain response before the promise will be fulfilled;
2. and, to promise is to perform a response: promising.

It is appropriate to equate promising with depriving, on the assumption that what is being promised is some object or event that an organism requires—one of the "goods" discussed previously. To present an organism with an opportunity to acquire such an object or event is, literally, to take that thing away from the organism. To hold out the prospect of getting something only after a behavioral event has been accomplished is, in every sense, a deprivational technique. The concept of deprivation as a promise-like set of conditions is not difficult to comprehend; the difficult part has been to see and accept that both depriving and promising are behaviors—in fact behaviors of another, potentially controlling organism.

I can initiate a causal sequence leading to a response by *II*, if *I* begins by promising something to *II*. Then *II* can acquiesce or refuse the promise, as confirmed by whether or not *II* performs the response in question. The choice presumably depends upon factors such as the appropriateness or attractiveness of the promise, the clarity with which it has been expressed, and/or the nature or degree of difficulty of the behavior the promise was designed to elicit.

Throughout this presentation of new theory intended to supplant that of the operant model, promising will designate a method by which an organism attempts to take control of another organism's behavior. This will be seen to be not, by far, the *only* means by which control of behavior is exercised. Other explanations will be presented, later in this book, to account for the many inter-relationships between organisms that can, in no way, be explained by promising alone. To translate depriving into promising serves to bring this method into sharper focus as one by which *human behavior* is controlled. There are many occasions in which one person makes an effort to obtain power over a second person through the device of offering certain "goods" and the implicit deprivation such an act intends.

What purpose does reinforcing serve? Reinforcing, to be most effective, will be carried out to an extent that does not equal the value of the original promise. This refers to the way in which partial reinforcement works. In a case in which the behavior of organism *II* is to be made to change gradually over repeated trials, more efficient results are obtained if reinforcement is presented only occasionally. The object is, in no case, to match the value involved in promising with the value provided by reinforcing. The reason for this is simple: when reinforcing *equals* promising, deprivation has been replaced by satiation.

Promising can be seen as a message by which organisms communicate. As a deprivational act, its sole object is to get another to do something. Once that something is done, reinforcing as a restorative act becomes the event at issue. Looked-at from the point of view of organism *I*, reinforcing to the value conveyed by prior promising is an act that reduces the potentiality of future control to zero. In order to control again, *I* will have to do more promising. On these terms, it is to the advantage of *I* to arrange reinforcing to provide a fractional measure of the amount promised originally. Looked-at from the point of view of organism *II*, reinforcing that equals promising constitutes a message that *II* has performed the precise behavior indicated. When this equilibrium of sought and obtained "goods" from the environment is not achieved, *II* has received a signal that the behavior performed was either not done often enough or was not exactly "correct" by some standard.

In summary, reinforcing an organism for its responses does not make sense unless depriving has first been done. To promise an organism and then, following the response, to reinforce the organism in keeping with the promise is to end a control relationship. To reinforce on a partial basis is to continue the control for an indefinite period. The length of this period will be determined by reinforcing behavior in relation to prior promising.

What happens above all in the typical operant demonstration is that, when reinforcement occurs, a kind of momentary break in the situation is provided. Following this break, an organism again must find a way to solve its problem—it is still deprived. Therefore, the organism will respond a second time and a third, etc.. Each time it responds, another break occurs in the cause/effect relationship; namely, a reinforcement appears. Reinforcement provided during the break has not altered the situation sufficiently to replace deprivation by satiation. The organism goes back to its deprivation-produced behavior. When seen from the point of view of its control by deprivation, the organism can be considered under one compulsion: to make responses. This is because the operant situation allows little compensation for each response made. The organism, being deprived, responds once; continuing to be deprived, it responds again. Now, why will these responses tend to be performed more and more rapidly? When the organism's responses do not produce sufficient reinforcement, what happens is that a prior period of deprivation is intensified. With the passage of time, a deprived organism becomes more deprived. If deprivation compels an organism to make responses, more intensive deprivation will cause it to make still more responses. It is thus not surprising that rate of behavior becomes more rapid under these circumstances. Psychology lore has it that the learning theorist Clark Hull (See Chapter II.) was bedeviled by a similar question to which he was not able to find an answer, namely: why does a horse, rented out for riding, run faster when returning to the barn than it did when leaving the barn? It does so because its deprivation has increased with the passage of time since leaving. Whether or not the animal ate in the barn before leaving, on leaving it entered into a condition of deprivation, with no prospect of relieving the condition until safely home. This Parable of the Fast-running Horse gives meaning to the term "horse sense."

When rat is placed in box, the only available information, at first, concerns a prevailing degree of deprivation. From this, it will be possible to explain numbers of responses to extinction. The observer can see rate of responding rise to an asymptotic level. It is clear that reinforcement does not act to cause this phenomenon, since it even occurs when reinforcement is absent from the sequence of events. Research by Brown and Jenkins helps to put this phenomenon in perspective (1968); they argued that " . . . in order to prove the necessity of reward in lever pressing, a control condition where food is delivered without regard to behavior must also be conducted. Skinner never published this control group. Only much later was it found that rats . . . do indeed learn to manipulate a lever when food comes irrespective of behavior. This phenomenon is known as autoshaping. Autoshaping demonstrates that consequence of action is not necessary in an operant conditioning chamber, and it contradicts the law of effect."

No-reinforcement is an extremely popular method of training domestic animals. It is called "clicker training," in which the sound of a clicker tells the animal that it has performed a response that was desired by the trainer. Initially paired with a food reinforcement, the sound of the clicker eventually is the only event that occurs after the desired response; the food has disappeared. The sound, of course, does nothing to assuage the animal's hunger, which means that prior deprivation is in no way weakened as a motivator of responding *per se*; its ultimate effect is to guide the animal to the "correct" response, by a process in which the animal can differentiate among potential responses. Thus *doing something* is caused by lack of food and doing a *particular thing* is taught by stimulus substitution (clicker for food) of the same sort achieved by Pavlov's metronome.

Some terms that have already been introduced, in this chapter, will prove useful in examining factors that are causal to *human* behavior. Since reinforcing and depriving are most appropriately considered behaviors themselves, the concepts of depriv*ing* and reinforc*ing* were worked out in previous analyses.

Just as depriving is analogous to promising, reinforcing can be shown to be following-through on a promise. The language of theory can be analyzed for this concept. The word "reinforcement" is compounded of the prefix "re" and "enforcement"; it means to enforce again. If to reinforce is to enforce for a second time, then prior promising is one method of enforcing behavior. The subject of behavioral enforcement—how it occurs and its significance for human conditioning—will be given full attention in the pages to follow.

A framework has been established for a principle of force as one which regulates behavior. The possibility of there being such a principle has been before Psychology from the time the concept of motivation was first considered in terms of extra-organismic events. That is, when the motive takes place *outside* organisms— in environments. The concept of the stimulus, in stimulus-response theories, was right for the wrong reasons: as structurally correct, it identified causes of behavior as environmental events; erring in content, it gave, as the causes of behavior, events which could not be called "motivating" in any sense of that term.

Once deprivation could be examined as behavior, the motive had been shifted to a place in the environment where it could be measured by the psychologist. The new locus for a motive was in the responses of another organism. When motivation had become motivating, and deprivation became depriving, a start had been made in solving the problem of the response as caused.

For a comprehensive theory of learning, an opening had developed that could only be bridged by a principle of force.

The next three chapters will describe, in detail, the concepts Promising (VI), Demonstrating (VII), and Commanding (VIII).

VI. PROMISING

The word "want" is in such common use that we rarely think about it when we use it. In fact, if your ear is attuned to it, you might hear it many times a day on the street, at work, and around the house.

There is an abstract meaning of "want," as when we refer to "a world without want." In a practical, everyday sense, it is synonymous with "lack." (i.e., "need"). When we say "I want," something is missing in our lives that we would like to have. This may seem mere semantics, but it means more in the context of how we learn, as this chapter sets forth.

Learning, defined as behavioral change, occurs in animals because the environment *creates* a lack. As an early behaviorist, Robert Thorndike confided, "So far as possible the animals were kept in a uniform state of hunger which was practically utter hunger." Given a means to sate its hunger, an animal does all it can to alleviate this lack: it acts with a purpose. The term "promising," used euphemistically to refer to depriving an animal, takes on new meaning when applied to the enforcement of *human* behavior. The correct term for this process is "incentive setting" (Two words are called-for because the noun "incentive" lacks a verb form; it can be traced in common usage to the 1940s.).

Incentive plans achieve results by *creating a need* to reach some goal or replace something that has been lost. When a worker is hired to do a job, the salary that is to be paid at, for example, the end of a month, has been "taken away" from the worker in advance; he or she is promised it and can only get it by doing a month's work. A lottery offers the player, for a small fee, an opportunity to win a large sum of money; when the ticket is bought, the player enters a state of being promised what could be won, the prize. In the beginning, of course, the person is not expected to do more than buy a ticket before the drawing is made; but, because in nearly every instance the prize will not be won, deprivation persists, the incentive remains, and the person is motivated to respond again with ticket-buying behavior.

Much of human activity strives to regain what has been lost, a search for homeostasis. Human beings, as with any life form, exist in a perpetual state of deprivation, only now and again relieved by the acquisition of some object or the occurrence of some event. They are rarely fully sated. The average person feels deprived of food two or three times a day, at least, and of sleep after approximately sixteen hours. An incentive system exploits these natural deficits. One is reminded of the saying of Proudhon, "Property is theft." What someone else has, you don't have and might have. People do what they do because something has been withheld from them or denied them. People climb Mount Everest because "it is there," and some seek the moon and sixpence. In short, they strive to alleviate deprivation. The more they obtain of what they lack, the fewer are their goal-seeking actions in frequency of occurrence, and when the need is fulfilled they move toward a state of abulia. A reward won is an incentive lost.

An example of this process, when a person is promoted from one level in a company to a higher one, as long as there is more "room at the top," incentive to work harder, smarter, more deviously, increases accordingly. To get what you've got casts light on what you haven't got. The race to the top goes on.

In another example, the first day on a job, a job in which there is, presumably, a chance for advancement, incentive is limitless. This process depends, again, on manipulation from forces in the person's environment (Incentive is set, not found.). Those who manipulate directly do it by withholding or granting fulfillment of the incentive previously set. In the extreme, poverty is the stick and wealth the carrot. It was ever thus, from time immemorial. For example, everyone in America *wants* to be a millionaire. Or, as a dear friend of mine once said, "Everyone wants to be above average."

In review of this and preceding chapters, deprivation motivates behavior, while reinforcement lessens motivation. The sole purpose of reinforcement is to guide behavior by providing information about the correct response, and this guidance is tempered by the corresponding risk of satiation. William James wrote that habit is "the enormous flywheel of society" (1890, p. 121). The great flywheel of learning is expressed by the phrase "I want." Want is the wellspring of action.

VII. DEMONSTRATING

Imitation is a powerful force in animal life. When Konrad Lorenz walked along with a flock of geese trailing after him, the geese followed *something* by instinct, but Lorenz showed them the route.

What this example means is that imitating is a primitive mode of learning. It has been hard-wired through evolution into a natural process of which we are not fully conscious, but occurs daily in our relations with others. The source of this process is the behavior of one person in a relationship whose actions create the actions of another. This source is called here "demonstrating."

A newborn child has no words. Naturally, he has an ever-broadening repertoire of sounds. Because everything he knows or will come to know will have been taught, his behavior is shaped by those around him who teach "Daddy" for "Da-da" and "Mommy" for "Ma-ma." Every spontaneous utterance is modified by correction. Each time the child speaks, the parent or caregiver corrects pitch, intonation, accent, etc. ("DaDDee"). The teachers of these fundamentals of speech do it without awareness that they do—it's reflexive. They need neither plan nor strategy. The child takes the lead by making his sounds and his teachers tell him how to say it.

When the child repeats a word and later attaches it to a thing or event or situation (e.g., hunger), it has learned; above all, the child has been taught. This learning was not originated by the child, nor did it arrive by some internal process: it was presented, shown, and then copied.

This mode of teaching is called, by some, "modeling." To be effective, this process requires that the modeling person (teacher) is capable of doing the modeling, willing to do it, and knows the subject well. Here, the word "demonstrating" refers to the same method as modeling. To invert an old saying, this approach amounts to "Don't do as I say, do as I do." Information about what behavior is to be done is taken in through observation. Demonstrating is the force and observation its medium.

Oddly enough, this force has a counterpart in the one practical application of operant theory to education: programmed teaching. What is a "program"? As with the tutorial method ascribed to Socrates, a program poses a series of questions on the topic to be learned, and indicates whether or not the answer is correct. Ideally, the sequence of questions is arranged so that a correct answer to one question contains a clue to the answer to another. When the text of a subject is presented in small, interlocking steps, called "frames," the pupil can move stepwise to an understanding of the concept being taught. If the steps presented are small enough, goes the theory, performance without error can be produced until complete mastery of the subject is reached.

There is no point in describing in detail this method of teaching, because it is no longer in use, but one example will show its inner workings. In an introductory program in a Psychology text, the pupil reads this statement: "A doctor taps your knee with a rubber hammer to test your _____." If the blank space on the screen is filled by "reflexes" by the pupil, the program responds with "correct." A few frames later, this sentence appears: "The stimulating object used by the doctor to elicit a knee jerk is a_____"; the correct answer is acknowledged by the program, and on to the next frame. What leads to correct responding is obvious; the program-writer (tutor, teacher) has *shown* the pupil how to respond. One step in the program is copied in the next. "Prompting" is the name for this modeling procedure in the lexicon of programming theory, referring in any case to the *behavior of the program-writer*.

This approach to learning uses the same principles as those of a father teaching his son to throw a baseball. One person demonstrates a concept or action and another copies it. This process of enforcing behavior is as natural as a ballet teacher showing a new move to a novice. Note that the causal force is not the demonstration but rather the *demonstrating*—itself a response. In teaching, the best question elicits the best answer. Socrates knew this full well.

In summary, learners learn because teachers teach. The teacher's own behavior is the stimulus, and the response is the learner's imitation. This process is primordial. In fact, early humans may have been inspired to do it by watching animals. Naturally, this is the means by which children learn language.

VIII. COMMANDING

The title of this chapter may strike the reader as unnecessarily harsh and overblown. Yet, with a subject as fundamental as how we learn, mincing words is uncalled-for. Each of us issues commands every day; "telling" is a euphemism, "asking" masks the behavior's intent, and "asking politely" is disingenuous. A common expression for this mode of teaching is "Do as I say, not as I do." There we have commanding in a nutshell.

Commanding, as one of the three forms of enforcing behavior described in this book, is part of the human condition and, as such, is neither right or wrong—it is.

When a sheepdog herds a flock of sheep by running around it and barking, he is telling the sheep what to do; that is, go in a certain direction. His job is to command their behavior. No significance is attached to this because the process is as natural as the sun rising in the East.

A classroom teacher knows very well that students learn from her commands. She seldom demonstrates the subject at hand, but rather puts it before the students and requires them to learn it. We can call this "rote learning," but, whatever we call it, Latin and calculus cannot be acquired any other way.

Being coerced to do or say something is offensive to all people some of the time and some people all of the time. A person's reaction to being controlled in this way is akin to the Freudian concept of "resistance." His attempt to draw thoughts and feelings and memories from the depths of the psyche was often met with silence or anger or both. People quickly weigh its positive and negative implications when told to do something by another. Some will resist on principle or, specifically, resist doing what is being commanded, but most will do some version of the behavior sought. Civilized society depends on this willingness to conform on the part of most human beings. If everyone had the spirit of the anarchist, chaos would ensue.

It's a good thing that people accept commands in some measure. When learning to drive a car, only the learner sits behind the wheel. The teacher barks orders to "Stay in your lane" or "Use your turn signals," and so on. Military discipline is invariably instilled by issuing commands and judging responses. Something in human nature makes us docile to this degree and acts as a saving grace. Because commanding is itself a response, the paradigm for human learning can be reduced to:

Figure 28.

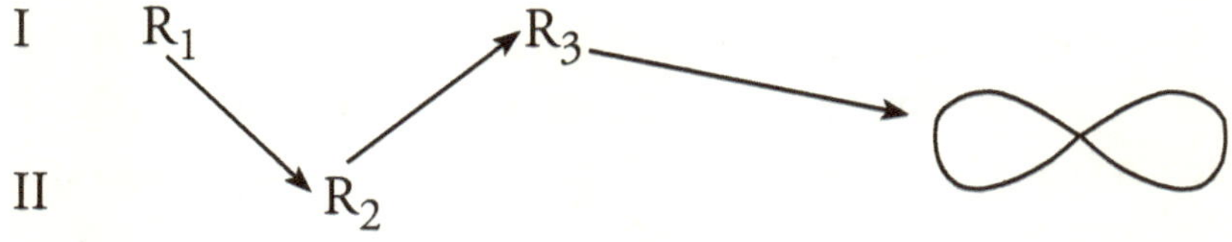

This paradigm conforms to Occam's Razor by its simplicity. It is a schematic formula for the elements of human interaction. It shows that the behavior of one person leads to the behavior of another, *ad infinitum*.

IX. OVERVIEW

Promising/demonstrating/commanding are arranged here in an ascending hierarchy of strength as causes of behavior. Promising contains more inherent disadvantages to the teacher than the others. For instance, promising entails either taking something away from the learner or holding out something desired but not yet received. To teach a child by withholding affection, the parent must convince the child that he or she has affection to be withheld. To control by withholding, one must first answer "What does he or she want?" The answer must be precise and entails specific knowledge of the person to be controlled.

Demonstrating requires, as described in Chapter VII, that the demonstrator do what the person who copies is being asked to do. The key to doing this is being aware of, and capable of adjusting, one's own behavior that will be copied. In nature, showing and imitating are facts of daily life. The lioness shows her cubs how to find prey and water and shelter. Absent this teaching behavior on the part of the mother, animals of nearly every species would founder and die. With people, it is often better to abandon demonstrating in favor of the more primitive method of promising or the more parsimonious method of commanding.

The premise of this analysis of learning is that learning requires interaction. The model for human learning, the core phenomenon, is the two-person interaction. Each of us learns through the agency of another, whether that person sets an incentive, models an action, or compels the action to occur.

A major flaw in the behaviorist exploration of learning was that the efforts of the experimenters to induce behavioral change were themselves responses. Their depriving and even their misguided reinforcing were just that—behavior. As such, it should have been acknowledged, analyzed, and incorporated into their theories. When the acts of one person lead to the acts of another, the event signifies as interaction. A series of interactions define a relationship. And the meaning of life is relationship (Everstine, 2000, 2007).

SUMMARY

These conclusions were drawn from the analysis presented in this book:

- a response has a discoverable cause
- a reinforcement (reward) does not affect the response that produced it
- less reinforcement is better than more
- reinforcing is a response
- depriving is a response
- reinforcing and depriving are antagonistic responses
- with humans, depriving is incentive-setting
- a reward is antagonistic to an incentive
- setting an incentive is a response
- people imitate what other people do
- showing someone what to do is a response
- people do what others tell them to do
- telling someone what to do is a response
- responses cause responses
- the medium of human learning is interaction

REFERENCES

Bateson, G. (1956) Toward a theory of schizophrenia. *Behavioral Science, 1,* 251-264.

Bateson, G. (1960) Minimal requirements for a theory of schizophrenia. *AMA Arch. Gen. Psychiatry, 2,* 477-491.

Boring, E. G. (1950) *A history of experimental psychology,* (second edition), New York: Appleton-Century-Crofts.

Boring, E. G. (1957) *A history of experimental psychology,* (third edition), New York: Appleton-Century-Crofts.

Brown, P. L. and Jenkins, H. M. (1968) Autoshaping of the Pigeon's Key-Peck. *J. Exp. Anal. Beh., 11,* 1-8.

Deese, J. (1958) *The psychology of learning,* (second edition). New York: McGraw-Hill.

Dennis, W. (1948) *Readings in the history of psychology,* New York: Appleton-Century-Crofts.

Dollard, J. and Miller, N. E. (1950) *Personality and psychotherapy,* New York: McGraw-Hill.

Everstine, L. (2000) *The Meaning of Life.* Philadelphia: Xlibris.

Everstine, L. (2007) *Life is Relationship.* Philadelphia: Xlibris.

Ferster, C. and Skinner, B. F. (1957) *Schedules of reinforcement*. New York: Appleton-Century-Crofts.

Findley, J. D. (1962) An experimental outline for building and exploring multi-operant behavior repertoires. *J. Exp. Anal. Beh., 5,* 113-166.

Grunbaum, A. (1953) Causality and the science of human behavior. In Feigl, H. and Brodbeck, May (Ed's) *Readings in the philosophy of science,* New York: Appleton-Century-Crofts.

Guthrie, E. R. (1935) *The psychology of learning*. New York: Harper.

Haley, J. (1959a) Control in psychoanalytic psychotherapy. In Masserman, J.H. and Moreno, J.L. (Ed's) *Progress in psychotherapy,* vol. IV. New York: Grune and Stratton.

Haley, J. (1959b) An interactional description of schizophrenia. *Psychiat., 22,* 321-332.

Haley, J. (1959c) The family of the schizophrenic: a model system. *J. Nerv. & Ment. Disease, 129,* 357-374.

Hebb, D. O. (1958) *A textbook of psychology*. Philadelphia: W.B. Saunders.

Hebb, D. O. (1960) The American revolution. *Amer. Psychol., 15,* 735-745.

Hilgard, E. R. and Marquis, D. G. (1940) *Conditioning and learning*. New York: Appleton-Century-Crofts.

Hilgard, E. R. (1956) *Theories of learning,* (second edition). New York: Appleton-Century-Crofts.

Hilgard, E. R. (1957) *Introduction to psychology,* (second edition). New York and Burlingame: Harcourt, Brace, and World.

Holland, J. G. and Skinner, B. F. (1961) *The analysis of behavior*. New York: McGraw-Hill

Hull, C. L. (1951) *Essentials of Behaviour*. Oxford: Oxford University Press

Hull, C. L. (1966) *Principles of Behavior.* New York: Appleton-Century-Crofts.

James, W. (1890) *The Principles of Psychology.* New York: Holt

Jackson, D. D. (1960) (Ed.) *The etiology of schizophrenia.* New York: Basic books.

Kelleher, R. T. and Gollub, L. R. (1962) A review of positive conditioned reinforcement. *J. Exp. Anal. Beh., 5,* 543-597.

Keller, F. S. and Schoenfeld, W. N. (1950) *Principles of psychology.* New York: Appleton-Century-Crofts.

Kohn, A. (1993) *Punished by Rewards.* Boston: Houghton Mifflin

Osgood, C. E. (1953) *Method and theory in experimental psychology.* New York: Oxford Univ. Press.

Pittenger, R. E., Hockett, C. F., and Danchy, J. J. (1960) *The first five minutes.* Ithaca, New York: Martineau.

Postman, L. (1947) Present status of the law of effect. *Psychol. Bull., 44,* 489-563.

Parker, B. (1971) *My Language Is Me.* New York: Ballantine Books.

Scriven, M. (1956) A study of radical behaviorism. In Feigl, H. and Scriven, M. (Ed's) *Minnesota studies in the philosophy of science.* Vol 1. Minneapolis: Univ. of Minnesota Press.

Sidman, M. (1960) *Tactics of scientific research.* New York: Basic Books.

Skinner, B. F. (1938) *The behavior of organisms.* New York: Appleton-Century-Crofts.

Skinner, B. F. (1947) Experimental psychology. In Dennis, W. (Ed.) *Current trends in psychology.* Pittsburgh: Univ. of Pittsburgh Press.

Skinner, B. F. (1950) Are theories of learning necessary? *Psychol. Rev., 57,* 193-216.

Skinner, B. F. (1953) *Science and human behavior.* New York: Macmillan.

Skinner, B. F. (1956) A case history in scientific method. *Amer. Psychol., 11,* 221-233.

Skinner, B. F. (1957) The experimental analysis of behavior. *Amer. Scientist, 45,* 343-371.

Skinner, B. F. (1957) *Verbal Behavior.* New York: Appleton-Century-Crofts.

Skinner, B. F. (1958) Reinforcement today. *Amer. Psychol., 13,* 94-99.

Skinner, B. F. (1960) Pigeons in a Pelican. *Amer. Psychol., 15,* 28-37.

Skinner, B. F. (1962) For Ivor Richards. *Encounter, 19,* 43, 44.

Spence, K. W. (1948) The methods and postulates of "behaviorism." *Psychol. Rev., 55,* 67-78.

Spence, K. W. (1956) *Behavior theory and conditioning.* New Haven: Yale Univ. Press.

Stevens, S. S. (1939) Psychology and the science of science. *Psychol. Bull., 36,* 221-263.

Thorndike, E. L. (1948) Animal intelligence. In Dennis, W. (Ed.) *Readings in the history of psychology.* New York: Appleton-Century-Crofts.

Tolman, E. C. (1932) *Purposive behavior in animals and men.* New York: Appleton-Century-Crofts.

Thorndike, E. L. (1903) *Educational Psychology.* New York: Lemecke and Buechnern

Verplanck, W. S. (1954) Burrhus F. Skinner. In Estes, W., *et al., Modern learning theory.* New York: Appleton-Century-Crofts.

Watson, J. B. (1930) *Behaviorism,* (revised edition). Chicago: Univ. of Chicago Press.

Wundt, W. (1902) *Outlines of psychology,* (second revised English edition). London: Williams and Margate.

INDEX

www.ingramcontent.com/pod-product-compliance
Lightning Source LLC
Chambersburg PA
CBHW020519290526
45786CB00002B/669